KT-389-463

PENGUIN  CLASSICS

THE SYMPOSIUM

ADVISORY EDITOR: BETTY RADICE

PLATO (*c.* 427–347 B.C.) stands with Socrates and Aristotle as one of the shapers of the whole intellectual tradition of the West. He came from a family that had long played a prominent part in Athenian politics, and it would have been natural for him to follow the same course. He declined to do so, however, disgusted by the violence and corruption of Athenian political life, and sickened especially by the execution in 399 of his friend and teacher Socrates. Inspired by Socrates' inquiries into the nature of ethical standards, Plato sought a cure for the ills of society not in politics but in philosophy, and arrived at his fundamental and lasting conviction that those ills would never cease until philosophers became rulers or rulers philosophers. At an uncertain date in the early fourth century B.C. he founded in Athens the Academy, the first permanent institution devoted to philosophical research and teaching, and the prototype of all western universities. He travelled extensively, notably in Sicily as political advisor to Dionysius II, ruler of Syracuse.

Plato wrote over twenty philosophical dialogues, and there are also extant under his name thirteen letters, whose genuineness is keenly disputed. His literary activity extended over perhaps half a century; few other writers have exploited so effectively the grace and precision, the flexibility and power, of Greek prose.

●

WALTER HAMILTON is an Honorary Fellow of Magdalene College, Cambridge, where he was also Master from 1967 until 1978. He was born in 1908 and was a Scholar of Trinity College, Cambridge, where he gained first class honours in both parts of the classical Tripos. He was a Fellow of Trinity College and a University Lecturer at Cambridge, and taught at Eton before becoming Headmaster of Westminster School (1950–57) and of Rugby School (1957–66). He has translated Plato's *Symposium*, the *Gorgias*, *Phaedrus* and *Letters VII and VIII* for Penguin Classics.

THE
SYMPOSIUM

PLATO

*

TRANSLATED BY
WALTER HAMILTON

PENGUIN BOOKS

Penguin Books Ltd, Harmondsworth, Middlesex, England
Viking Penguin Inc., 40 West 23rd Street, New York, New York 10010, U.S.A.
Penguin Books Australia Ltd, Ringwood, Victoria, Australia·
Penguin Books Canada Limited, 2801 John Street, Markham, Ontario, Canada L3R 1B4
Penguin Books (N.Z.) Ltd, 182–190 Wairau Road, Auckland 10, New Zealand

—

This translation first published 1951
Reprinted 1952, 1956, 1959, 1961, 1962, 1965, 1966, 1967,
1970, 1971, 1972, 1973, 1974, 1975, 1976,
1977, 1978, 1979, 1980 (twice), 1981, 1982, 1983, 1984, 1985, 1986, 1987

—

—

Printed and bound in Great Britain by
Cox & Wyman Ltd, Reading
Set in Monotype Caslon

CONTENTS

INTRODUCTION

INTRODUCTION

In the literary form known as dramatic dialogue Plato has no rival, ancient or modern, and of all his dialogues the *Symposium* or *Dinner-party* is the most varied and the most perfectly finished. It is also the least technical of the great works of his maturity; the philosopher in Plato has not yet banished the artist and the poet, and nowhere else, save in the *Phaedo* and perhaps in the *Protagoras*, has he devoted such care to the setting in which he frames his conversation-piece. The conversation, dealing as it does with love, is itself of universal interest, but the pictures which are presented to us of Athenian social life and of the character of Socrates are almost more fascinating, and the two elements are welded together with such consummate art that to dissect them is likely to destroy the perfect balance of the whole. Yet the risk must be run if the dialogue is to be made intelligible, and in what follows the *mise-en-scène*, the content of the conversation, and the character of Socrates will be separately discussed, though an attempt will be made to indicate how these various themes are interwoven with complete apparent naturalness so as to shed light reciprocally upon one another.

I

Such evidence as there is for the date of the composition of the dialogue points to a period not earlier than 385 B.C., but the time of the party of which it purports to give an account is securely fixed in 416 B.C. by its connexion with the dramatic triumph of the host, Agathon. That the conversation which takes place at it is fictitious cannot seriously be doubted, but Plato has been at unusual pains to impart to the whole scene a deceptive air of authority. The direct speakers are only two in number, Apollodorus and an unnamed friend, to whom among others Apollodorus reports at second-hand and many years after the event, though before the death of Socrates in 399 B.C., an account which he has had of the party from a member of Socrates' circle called Aristodemus, who was actually present at it. Since one of the main objects of the dialogue is to praise Socrates, it is clear that Socrates himself cannot be the narrator, but that in itself hardly explains the use of such curiously elaborate machinery. The effect is much the same as that given by Boswell when he reports some incident in Johnson's life which took place before their meeting, and just as Boswell often states that he has confirmed what he tells us by direct application to Johnson, so Apollodorus asserts that he has questioned Socrates on some points in Aristodemus' account. Plato's motive in all this seems to be to heighten the plausibility of his historical fiction by appealing to the authority of apparently unimpeachable witnesses; both Apollodorus and Aristodemus are historical persons, whom we know from other sources to have been fanatical admirers of Socrates.

So too, the guests named as having been present at Agathon's party are real people, and the whole atmosphere is such as we may readily believe to have existed among the upper classes at Athens in 416 B.C., when nothing had yet occurred to impair the mood of carefree and almost insolent superiority which found its supreme expression in Alcibiades. A year later his ambition was to lead his city into the disastrous adventure of the Sicilian expedition, which began the long death-agony of the Athenian Empire and involved him in dishonour and ruin; but no hint of this is allowed to intrude, and the picture of Alcibiades in the last scene of the dialogue, brilliant, charming, and completely shameless, for all that it must be an imaginative reconstruction, is as valuable evidence for his character and for the nature of the spell which he cast over his contemporaries as the substance of what he says is for the character of Socrates.

At this point a brief account of the structure of the dialogue may be helpful. Aristodemus meets Socrates on his way to dine with Agathon, a tragic poet, who is celebrating his recent success in the dramatic competition. Socrates takes Aristodemus with him, but does not arrive till the meal is half over. Eryximachus, a doctor, whose fussy officiousness is portrayed with admirable humour, then proposes that instead of the usual entertainment by flute-girls the company shall amuse itself with talk, and that this shall take the form of a speech from each member of the company in praise of love. His proposal is adopted, and the main section of the dialogue consists of speeches delivered by Phaedrus, who is said to be the real author of the idea, Pausanias, who according to Xenophon was notorious for his devotion to Agathon, Eryximachus himself, Aristophanes, the great comic poet, Agathon, and Socrates, with interludes between them. At the conclusion of Socrates' speech a commotion is heard outside, and Alcibiades enters with some drunken companions and is warmly welcomed. The party becomes much less decorous; Alcibiades takes the lead, and, when he is invited to contribute to the original scheme, declares that the only subject on which he is willing to make a laudatory speech is Socrates. He proceeds to give at some length a sketch of the character of Socrates and of his own relations with him. Finally a fresh party of revellers bursts into the house; all restraint is cast aside; some of the guests become incapable, others go home, and Aristodemus falls asleep. When he awakes towards morning he finds only Agathon, Aristophanes, and Socrates still drinking and talking; shortly afterwards the two former succumb, and Socrates leaves as fresh and sober as when he arrived, with Aristodemus still in attendance.

II

The kernel of the dialogue is of course the speech of Socrates, but the earlier speeches, each of which is strongly individual, and most of which are probably parodies of the styles of their supposed speakers, are so arranged as each to contribute something to the philosophy of love expounded by Socrates. But before indicating briefly the points which Socrates takes up or corrects in the earlier speeches, and trying to show the relation of the contents of his speech to the rest of Plato's philosophy, we must first face a fact which is so repugnant to the orthodox morality of our own times that there is a serious risk of its destroying the value and pleasure of the *Symposium* for many readers. The love with which the dialogue is concerned, and which is accepted as a matter of course by all the speakers, including Socrates, is homosexual love; it is assumed without argument that this alone is capable of satisfying a man's highest and noblest aspirations, and the love of man and woman, when it is mentioned at all, is spoken of as altogether inferior, a purely physical impulse whose sole object is the procreation of children. In approaching the *Symposium* we must set aside our personal views as irrelevant and accept this state of affairs as an historical fact, if we are to achieve much understanding either of this aspect of Plato's thought or of the character of Socrates.

It is generally held that, apart from a few brilliant exceptions like Aspasia, the mistress of Pericles, women in the golden age of Greece, both at Athens and in other states, took no part in public life and hardly any in public amusements, and that their confinement to the domestic affairs of their homes at a period when a citizen spent almost his whole life out of doors made it impossible for them to become adequate companions to their husbands. Where young persons of opposite sexes rarely met, marriage would normally be merely a matter of arrangement and romantic love impossible. Whether this is an altogether satisfactory account of the relations between the sexes seems at least open to question, and it is still more doubtful whether in any case it provides a sufficient explanation of the homosexual tendency of Athenian men. The part played by women in tragedy does not suggest complete inferiority and seclusion, and it may be that our belief in the prevalence of homosexuality is exaggerated by the fact that it was free from the necessity of concealment which later moral codes have imposed upon it. But that it was not uncommon, at any rate among the leisured classes, is undeniable, and it would certainly appear that the conception of marriage as a partnership between man and woman for all the purposes of life was almost entirely foreign to the Greek mind. Even Plato, who in the *Republic* proposes that men and women shall receive exactly the same education and be equally capable of discharging all the duties of a citizen, at the same time expressly prohibits for the men and women of his ruling class anything beyond temporary sexual relations for the purpose of breeding. It is true that both there and in the *Laws* he forbids also sexual intercourse between men, and condemns it as being unnatural, but this is probably due more to a puritanical aversion from the physical aspect of sex in any form than to a disapproval of homosexuality as such, and he certainly seems to have held that a homosexual relationship is alone capable of being transformed into a lifelong partnership, and that homosexual love, like heterosexual love with us, has a range which extends from the crudest physical passion to a marriage of noble minds with no physical manifestation at all. The earlier speeches in the *Symposium* deal with various gradations in this scale, and the ideal is finally put forward, and sensuality entirely transcended and sublimated, in the speech of Socrates.

The first two speakers, Phaedrus and Pausanias, confine themselves to the treatment of love in its most obvious sense. And here it should perhaps be observed that the personification of Love which persists throughout the dialogue, though often little more than a figure of speech, is a further fact for which allowance must be made by an English reader, unaccustomed to such a manner of treating psychology and metaphysics. To Phaedrus the nature of Love presents no difficulties; he is the oldest of the gods, and the supreme benefactor of mankind, inspiring both a high sense of honour, because a man is particularly afraid of being detected by his lover or beloved in any mean or cowardly action, and also the spirit of self-sacrifice. These conclusions are illustrated by examples from history and mythology, and woman, in the person of Alcestis, is allowed a place in the category of those who may be led to sacrifice their lives by love.

Pausanias, though hardly more profound, is a good deal more subtle, and introduces a distinction between a nobler and a baser kind of love which in a sense prepares the way for Socrates. The baser love aims at nothing beyond sensual gratification; it finds the means to this in women and young boys, and in the latter case it is to be severely discouraged. The nobler love is directed exclusively towards young men, and its object is a lifelong association productive of such good results as have been described by Phaedrus. In the light of this distinction the attitude of various states and forms of government towards homosexuality is analysed, and the apparent inconsistency of public opinion on the subject at Athens explained. But the importance of the distinction drawn by Pausanias should not blind us to the fact that the nobler sort of love no more precludes sexual relations than the baser, and it is possible to see in Pausanias a clever pleader for homosexual licence, who employs high-sounding but sophistical reasoning to justify the satisfaction of physical desire. His principle that all actions are morally indifferent in themselves, and becomes good or bad only through their circumstances or motives, particularly lays him open to this charge, and is fundamentally opposed to the teaching of Plato.

Pausanias should be succeeded by Aristophanes, but Aristophanes is suffering from a hiccup, and Eryximachus prescribes for this and takes Aristophanes' turn. Eryximachus is very strongly and cruelly drawn in the narrative part of the dialogue as a pompous and oracular pedant, and the speech which is put into his mouth is characteristic of him. He is unable to consider any subject except in a professional and technical way, and the main idea in his speech, the distinction between a good and a bad kind of love, is not original, but borrowed from Pausanias. His method is to exalt this distinction into a universal principle, whose operation may be detected not only in the human soul, but also in his own study, medicine, and even in music, astronomy, and divination. His analysis of these activities in the light of this principle is mechanical, catalogue-like, and forced, and must have seemed so even to readers to whom the scientific theories on which he relies were living and credible. He is ready to torture the most diverse phenomena into the strait-waistcoat of a single formula quite arbitrarily assumed, and it can be no accident that in his treatment of music he is made to misinterpret a famous theory of Heraclitus.

Yet, though Eryximachus' speech is poor stuff and meant to be so – it is presumably by way of contrast that it is interposed between the much more important speeches of Pausanias and Aristophanes – it has its contribution to make to the whole. The treatment of love as a cosmic principle at work in the universe at large, though pushed by Eryximachus to the point of absurdity, marks a significant transition from the narrow sense of physical desire which is all that it has been given by Phaedrus and Pausanias, and to that extent prepares the reader for the ascent from physical to intellectual love and from the sensible to the ideal world which will be described by Socrates.

Eryximachus ends with a self-satisfied invitation to Aristophanes to fill up any gaps that he may have left in his speech, 'unless you plan to take some other line in praising the god'.

It is like Eryximachus to be insensitive to the absurdity of expecting a mind so richly inventive and whimsical as that of Aristophanes to be content to follow his own pedestrian and mechanical method; in fact the contrast between them is overwhelming, and the speech which Plato assigns to Aristophanes constitutes almost the most brilliant of all his achievements as a literary artist. Beginning with a humorous fantasy of the nature of the first human beings and of their rebellion against the gods, which has often been called Rabelaisian and which recaptures much of the spirit of Aristophanes' own comedy of the *Birds*, the speech goes on to describe man's present condition. Men are merely halves of original wholes, which were of three sexes, male, female, and hermaphrodite, and were bisected by Zeus as a punishment for their pride. Love is 'the desire and pursuit of the whole', man's attempt to regain his former happy state by uniting himself to his lost half, and the direction taken by the sexual impulse in any individual is dictated by the nature of the whole to which that individual originally belonged. It is noteworthy that Aristophanes, unlike the other speakers, treats heterosexual and homosexual love as being on the same level, since both are predestined; but this is an inevitable consequence of the mythical hypothesis of three original sexes, and we cannot infer from it any real change of attitude, especially as Aristophanes is made to describe as the best among their contemporaries those individuals who are halves of male wholes and in consequence homosexual.

Aristophanes speaks of himself as merely an entertainer, and his speech begins as a *jeu d'esprit* of fantasy in whose details we need not expect to find any very profound meaning, but, as he continues, a vein of seriousness and almost of pathos begins to mingle with the humour, and an important truth is brought to light. Aristophanes recognizes that love is a need, and a need whose satisfaction is much more than physical; the nature of this universal need or desire will be explored and explained to Socrates by Diotima. But love is also a longing to regain a lost happiness, and this too is characteristic of Platonic love at its highest. The ultimate object of love is the vision of absolute beauty which man's soul once enjoyed before it was incarnate, when in the language of the myth in the *Phaedrus* it followed in the procession of the gods upon the 'plain of truth'.

An interlude of some length follows, apparently designed to create an atmosphere of heightened expectation for the speech of Agathon. None of Agathon's plays survives, but the picture which is drawn of him in the *Symposium* and confirmed by what is known from other sources is not so much of a professional writer as of a dilettante, handsome, elegant, and vain, recognizably akin to the decadents of other ages and countries. His speech is what one might expect from such a person, a rhetorical exercise composed according to the rules of the sophist Gorgias, the emptiness and preciosity of which stand in strong contrast with the speeches both of Aristophanes and of Socrates. Aristophanes, the comic poet, delivers in simple, unaffected language a speech which, for all its extravagance of fancy, has an underlying strain of strong and genuine feeling; Agathon, the tragic poet, beneath his carefully elaborated style and consciously poetical diction, is at his best cold, superficial, and conventional, and at his worst a mere verbal trickster, as when he proves that Love must be self-controlled because he is master of all the passions.

More important is the contrast with Socrates. Rhetoric and philosophy are here face to face, the former content if its conceits tickle the ear and using the theme proposed merely as a foundation on which to build its artificial edifice of words and rhythms, the latter labouring to discover the truth and professing indifference to its formal expression, though in fact Plato is too thorough an artist for Socrates' speech not to be perfect in form. Agathon claims to improve upon the methods of his predecessors, who have talked of the gifts conferred by Love rather than of his essential nature, but his own method is simply to heap upon Love all desirable qualities and all virtues, and he closes with a tremendous purple passage, of which Socrates subsequently remarks that the beauty of its words and phrases (not, be it noted, of its thought) has taken his breath away. Even Agathon is allowed to contribute one positive idea, that the object of love is beauty, but otherwise the importance of his speech is purely negative, in that it provides material upon which Socrates' dialectic may work in order to establish certain preliminary conclusions.

The discussion between Agathon and Socrates which follows arises so naturally from Agathon's speech that it would be easy not to notice that we are here entering on the second and much the more important section of the dialogue. The transition is marked by a significant change of tone. Socrates with characteristic irony professes to be overwhelmed with admiration at what he has heard, and exclaims that he would never have been so foolish as to put himself in competition with the others in praising Love had he known that what is needed in a panegyric is not knowledge of the nature of its object but a flow of fine phrases and laudatory language whether true or false. As it is, he must withdraw from the contest; he is willing, however, to make a plain statement of the truth about Love, provided that it is understood that he is not competing. This is the answer of the philosopher to the rhetorician; in what follows we shall be engaged, not with prize exercises upon a set theme, but with the search for truth. What more natural then than that Socrates should begin by employing upon Agathon the instrument of philosophical inquiry that is peculiarly his own, the method of question and answer, of which the first stage consists in reducing the interlocutor to 'helplessness', the admission that his existing views upon the subject under discussion are completely mistaken?

The criticism is sometimes made that Socrates often overcomes his opponents in such discussions by methods which seem to us unfair and quibbling, but in Agathon's case, at any rate, the argument appears to be quite legitimate. The positions established are: (1) that Love is a relative name like Father or Mother, and implies the existence of an object loved: (2) that Love (or at least that form of love which the Greeks called *Eros*) desires his object: (3) that desire is not felt for what is already possessed: (4) that since the object of Love, on Agathon's own showing, is beauty, Love cannot be beautiful, nor, since, as he also agrees, the good is the same as the beautiful, can he be good. This paradoxical conclusion is the result of no mere word-play. The point is established that love is the consciousness of a need for a good not yet acquired or possessed. A hint of this has already been given in Aristophanes' fantasy, but it is now laid down on rational grounds as a foundation for the exposition of Plato's own view.

Agathon admits that he did not know what he was talking about, and Socrates embarks upon his promised statement, which, however, takes the curious form of a reported debate between Socrates and a woman of Mantinea called Diotima, who plays the same part towards Socrates as Socrates himself has just been playing towards Agathon. It is almost universally and no doubt rightly held that Diotima is a fictious personage, in spite of the apparently historical statements made about her by Socrates. It is not desirable here to go into the arguments in favour of this conclusion, but it may be noticed that this is not the only place in the Platonic dialogues where Socrates is made to ascribe the substance of what he has to say to others, particularly in dealing with subjects such as love and the fate of the soul about which dialectically established certainty is impossible, and that it was precisely with regard to such subjects that Plato was most influenced by the mystery religions of his day, whose language is here used by Diotima in describing the ascent of the soul from the sensible to the eternal world. If we ask what was Plato's purpose in using this device on the present occasion, it may suffice for the moment to answer that it is more consistent with the amenity of the party, and softens the rough handling which Agathon has just received, that Socrates should be placed on the same level as the rest of the company and not represented as a hierophant revealing ultimate truth; the tone used by Diotima to him is very much that of sage to pupil, and she is even made to express a doubt whether he will be capable of the final initiation into the mysteries of love.

Socrates, then, reports that he has been convinced by the same arguments as he has just used against Agathon that Love is neither good nor beautiful, and proceeds to give the rest of his supposed conversation with Diotima. It does not follow that because Love is neither good nor beautiful he is therefore ugly and bad. He is in an intermediate state, just as a man who has true opinions without being able to give a rational account of them is half-way between wisdom and ignorance. This comparison is of supreme importance for the understanding of the dialogue. It presupposes the whole of Plato's Theory of Ideas or Forms, which, reduced to its barest elements, is that the manifold and ever-changing phenomena of the world of sense are imitations or copies of eternal and absolute Forms, which alone have true reality, and to 'participation' in which the sensible world owes such partial reality as it possesses. The impulse to this theory was originally given by the search of the historical Socrates for universal definitions of moral concepts, but the mature system goes far beyond anything that Socrates can be supposed to have contemplated; apparently for almost every class of things, whether material or abstract, which can be embraced under a common name, there exists a Form in the eternal world. The task of the philosopher is to pass from the shadows of the sensible world, by which he is 'reminded' of the Forms, which the soul saw before its incarnation, to the contemplation of the realities of the Forms themselves. These are arranged in a hierarchy, at the head of which stands the Form of Good, and the man who has made this ascent and who can see reality as a connected system dependent upon this Form has wisdom; all others have at the best only true opinion. The ascent demands the severest intellectual training, the stages of which are described in the central books of the *Republic*; but it is another aspect of the same ascent which is described by Diotima in the *Symposium*, because, as we have been told in the argument with Agathon, the beautiful and the good coincide, and it is the beautiful that is the object of love. The philosopher who makes the purely intellectual pilgrimage of the *Republic* is also the ideal lover of the *Symposium*, who is led by examples of beauty in the world of sense to the same goal, the contemplation of the Form of Beauty, a mystical experience which is incommunicable, but which Plato comes nearest to describing in the concluding passage of the speech of Diotima. Love, therefore, the consciousness of need for the beautiful and the good, is not beautiful and good because it has not attained its goal, but in so far as it is an attempt to strive towards it, it is removed from the opposite state of being ugly and bad.

Love, in fact, as Diotima goes on to show, is one of the links between the sensible and the eternal world. This is expressed mythologically by making him a being of intermediate nature between gods and men, one of the class known to the Greeks as spirits or daemons, and the idea of the contrarieties in his nature is reinforced by a myth of his birth. Poverty was his mother, and he therefore lives in want, but from his father, Contrivance, he has inherited boldness and resourcefulness in pursuing his object. He is a philosopher or lover of wisdom, because wisdom is beautiful and beauty is the object of Love. And here it may be remarked that the lover too, and indeed man in general, is a daemon, a creature attached to both worlds, and Plato's analysis of man's condition appears to be consistent with religious experience. Life is a struggle for a far-away but dimly discerned good, to attain which is happiness. If man possessed it he would no longer be man; if he had no yearning for it he would be mere animal. What Plato calls ignorance Christians call sin, but this apparently fatal discrepancy fades in the light of the Socratic and Platonic doctrine that all wrong-doing is ignorance, and that perfect knowledge inevitably issues in perfect conduct.

If love embraces every desire for good and for happiness, all men may be called lovers, and we seem to have wandered far indeed from the common man's idea of love. Diotima explains that, though in the widest sense all men are lovers of the good (or what they conceive to be such), yet in ordinary usage the name Eros has been restricted to the sense of sexual love, the meaning which has been attributed to it by all the previous speakers. This is one form of desire for the good, and here the important point is introduced without argument that men desire not merely to possess the good but to possess it perpetually. There is only one way in which Eros in the narrow sense can achieve anything like perpetuity, and that is by procreation. Through the perpetual replacement of an old member of the race by a new, mortal creatures can put on immortality, and so procreation, for which association with beauty is a necessary condition, may be said to be the natural object of love.

Although Diotima appears thus to restrict the range of the discussion to sexual love, it at once becomes plain that this restriction is illusory. Physical procreation is only one, and that the lowest, of the forms which Eros can take. Far nobler is spiritual procreation, the activity of the soul to which we owe not only the products of art but all progress in civilization and the ordering of society. All such advances are apparently to be attributed to the marriage of noble minds; when a man's soul is pregnant with some creation or discovery he looks for a partner in association with whom he may bring his spiritual offspring to birth. Physical beauty will influence his choice of such a partner, but the marriage will not be fertile unless there is also beauty of soul.

We seem to have arrived again at the nobler of the two kinds of homosexuality distinguished by Pausanias, and this may cause surprise in view of the previous conclusion that the object of love is procreation, and that even in animals what appears to be a desire for sexual union is really desire for parenthood. One might have expected that this would lead to an unequivocal condemnation of homosexuality as being sterile. The reason why it does not do so is that for Plato physical parenthood is the lowest and least important kind – he is not really concerned with it at all – and spiritual parenthood, with very rare exceptions, is possible only for men. In spite of the emphasis laid on the equality of the sexes in the ideal state of the *Republic* he presumably believed that, as things are, women are incapable of creative activity above the physical level. So what might well have been a strong argument for heterosexuality is with Plato an argument for a refined homosexuality, though, as we shall see shortly, it is a homosexuality which in its highest form is entirely unphysical.

So far, then, we have advanced only one stage beyond physical parenthood, and it is to be noticed that the examples which Diotima gives of persons in whom love has taken the form of desire to leave an immortal name behind them, Alcestis, Achilles, Codrus, are not chosen from among philosophers. Even when she passes on to those in whom it is easier to recognize spiritual parenthood by reason of their tangible achievements still remaining with us, she does not rise above poets and lawgivers. It is at this point that she expresses the doubt already mentioned of Socrates' ability to follow her further, and this marks a critical stage in the argument. Henceforth she is concerned with a third and even nobler type of lover, the philosopher or lover of wisdom, who is capable of ascending above the sensible world altogether. The stages of his ascent are from love of particular examples of physical beauty to physical beauty in general; thence to beauty of soul even if unaccompanied by beauty of body (in this he is distinguished from the second type of lover already described), and so to moral beauty in general; and finally to the beauty of knowledge, and through various branches of knowledge to that vision of the Form of Beauty itself which gives complete and unifying knowledge of truth concerning the whole universe. This is the same intellectual pilgrimage as is described in the *Republic*; what we have added to it here (and in the *Phaedrus*) is the idea that it is a pilgrimage inspired by love. Diotima describes it in terms borrowed from the mysteries, partly, no doubt, because it is a gradual progress comparable to the stages of an initiation, and partly because the final vision is a religious rather than an intellectual experience, and, like the culminating revelation of a mystery religion, is not to be described or communicated. The guide of the desiring soul corresponds to the hierophant of the mysteries, but we shall hardly be wrong to see in him also the familiar features of Socrates, practising what he calls in the *Theaetetus* his art of 'midwifery', by which he helps his associates to bring to birth the ideas and discoveries with which they are in travail.

There follows a description of the life of the lover of wisdom who has made this ascent. He has absolutely emancipated himself from the bonds of sense, and lives in the real and not the perishable world: we may fitly compare Diotima's final words with the description given of such blessedness in a corresponding passage of the *Republic* (490): 'Shall we not reasonably plead that the genuine lover of learning has a natural tendency to strive towards true being, and does not remain among the multiplicity of particular things which men believe to be real? On the contrary he goes on his way with unabated desire and unceasing love until he can lay hold of the real nature of each thing with that part of the soul which can lay hold of reality because it is akin to it. Then and not till then, when he has approached reality and entered into union with it and begotten intelligence and truth, does he enjoy knowledge and true life and nourishment, and cease from the pangs of travail.' Here also we find Plato using the language of love, and speaking of the crowning achievement of the philosophic quest as a marriage with the supremely real and good.

The understanding of the *Symposium* has sometimes been hampered by failure to recognize the vital distinction between the second and third types of lover. Comparison with the *Phaedrus*, which is also largely concerned with the subject of love, confirms the existence of the distinction, if confirmation is needed. There too we are presented with the same three types, the purely sensual, those who are called in the *Phaedrus* 'lovers of honour', and the lovers of wisdom. The second type, who have not entirely passed beyond physical love, and who correspond to the nobler lovers of Pausanias, are not condemned in either dialogue; in the *Phaedrus* it is positively stated that these lovers are capable of growing wings which may lift them again into the eternal world of the Forms which the soul once inhabited. Such lovers may have trouble in subduing their physical desires, and may never rise above the level of the 'lover of honour', but they are infinitely to be preferred to the merely sensual lover, who is severely indicted, and they have made some progress towards the state from which they fell at birth. The best type, however, the lover of wisdom, though he may still feel some pleasure in the things of sense, will never allow them to divert him for an instant from the pursuit of real beauty. But it is to be remembered that the first impulse to that pursuit, even in his case, is provided by the physical beauty of particular persons. Plato's opinions, when he wrote these two dialogues, had not yet crystallized into the complete reprobation of all physical homosexuality which we find in the *Laws*, and there can be little doubt that he, as well as Socrates, was strongly attracted by beautiful young men. Socrates frequently speaks of himself as being in love with them, and we must recognize that such language is not wholly ironic; the irony consists in such love having a meaning for him quite different from that which the common man attaches to it. Such considerations lead us to the final scene of the dialogue, the speech of Alcibiades in praise of Socrates.

First, however, a few final words on the Platonic theory of love as expounded by Diotima. An attempt has been made to show, very superficially, that it is an integral part of Plato's whole philosophical system. Eros is for him a principle pervading all worthy human activities, and Platonic love, in spite of the meaning commonly attributed to it, is a common search for truth and beauty by two persons of the same sex inspired by mutual affection. Plato's conviction is that it is the same impulse which prompts love between individuals (provided that it is something more than mere physical desire) and the search of the philosopher for truth or, we might add, of the mystic for God. The extended range of meaning thus given to the term 'love' seemed no doubt paradoxical to most of his original readers, and may well seem so to us. Even if we leave out of account the fact that for Plato true love between individuals is normally homosexual, it is not easy to follow him even as far as the second section of his first stage, the generalized love of physical beauty. After that what Plato calls love is hardly what we recognize as love at all, especially when he speaks of the moral beauty of laws and institutions as objects of love. Yet two considerations may be urged in favour of Plato's theory. First, modern psychology has detected the operation of the sexual impulse in many hitherto unsuspected fields, and viewed as the gradual sublimation of physical desire the ascent described by Diotima may sound more plausible to modern ears than to those of the Greeks. Secondly, the terms in which Plato speaks of the felicity of the lover of wisdom when he has achieved what we may not unreasonably call the beatific vision is much the same as that which has been found appropriate by mystics of other ages and countries; we have only to think, for example, of the interpretation which Christianity has placed upon the *Song of Solomon*, and of the countless instances in mystical writings in which the individual soul, no less than the Church, is spoken of as the bride of Christ.

III

It is a violent transition from the sublimity of Socrates-Diotima to the drunken antics of Alcibiades, but the change is purely a change of tone; no change of subject is involved in Alcibiades' declaration that, if he is to follow the others and deliver a panegyric, the only possible subject for it is Socrates. Socrates is for Plato the perfect example of the lover of wisdom; Alcibiades calls him 'daemon-like', and it is hardly going too far to regard him as Eros incarnate; the most superficial reading reveals that in describing his character and way of life Plato is simply clothing in flesh and blood the sketch of Eros at work in the soul of the true philosopher already drawn by Diotima. This suggests another and weightier reason than that given above for the introduction of Diotima into the dialogue; it would be a violation of dramatic tact to put directly into the mouth of Socrates praise of a type of character of which he is himself shortly to provide the complete illustration; it would come dangerously near involving him in a panegyric of himself. Yet Socrates, as the leading figure of the dialogue, must make the speech which is the pivot of the whole; hence the device of making that speech a reported conversation, and the emphasis laid throughout upon Socrates' position as pupil. Though he fulfils Plato's conception of the ideal he does so unconsciously, and in thus representing him Plato remains faithful to fundamental historical fact.

Socrates, like Eros, is full of contradictions; spiritual beauty is allied in him to physical ugliness, and the appearance of a Satyr conceals a wonderful self-control, which makes him utterly indifferent to pleasure, hardship, and danger.

Alcibiades illustrates these characteristics by anecdotes of events in Socrates' life, such as his celebrated trance at Potidaea (to which his behaviour on the way to Agathon's party provides a parallel on a smaller scale) and his courage on the retreat from Delium. But the supreme example of his mastery of sensual appetites is his resistance to Alcibiades' attempt to seduce him. We are not to suppose that he is not tempted, but he sets aside Alcibiades' charms as being of less value than the moral and intellectual beauty after which he is striving, and in this he shows himself the noblest kind of lover, who has passed beyond the love of physical beauty though he is still sensible of its attractions.

So far all is straightforward, but there is a complementary aspect of the relations of Socrates with Alcibiades. Whereas on the physical plane Socrates is the lover and Alcibiades the beloved, even though Socrates refrains from any gratification of physical desire, on the spiritual plane the rôles are reversed. Alcibiades finds its hard to explain the nature of the attraction which Socrates exercises over him, the effect of which is to make him feel dissatisfied with himself and ashamed of his present way of life, but in terms of Diotima's doctrine it is clear that what draws him to Socrates is beauty of soul. As the possessor of this, Socrates is the beloved, and Alcibiades is sufficiently highly gifted to be in love with him for this reason. He is not, however, prepared to abandon himself to the consequences of this feeling, which would involve a complete conversion from his career of dissipation and political ambition; he attempts to win Socrates' affection by the offer of his own physical charms – an endeavour, no doubt, to quiet his uneasy conscience by proving to himself that Socrates is no better than other people. When this fails, he is left in a state of mingled irritation and attraction; he cannot tear himself away from Socrates, but he continues to kick against the pricks, unfortunately both for him and for Socrates with a thoroughness which the very brilliance of his endowments makes all the more complete. The best commentary on such a situation is provided by Plato himself in the *Republic* (494), where, no doubt with Alcibiades in mind, he shows that it is the most promising natures which go most disastrously wrong if they succumb to the temptation offered by public life. Alcibiades' condition may in fact be excellently summed up in the famous words *Video meliora proboque, deteriora sequor*, and it seems odd that, faced with the example of his conscious rejection of the higher for the lower, both Socrates and Plato should have remained unshaken in their profound belief that all wrong-doing is the result of ignorance.

However that may be, it is not to be doubted that one object of the *Symposium* in general and of Alcibiades' speech in particular is to make plain that Socrates was in no way responsible for Alcibiades' betrayal of his country in the Peloponnesian War two years after the dramatic date of the dialogue. It had been one of the main charges against Socrates at his trial that he had corrupted several of the most prominent and talented young Athenians by his conversation, and led them to abandon traditional morality and embark upon courses subversive of the Athenian democracy. The fact that an act of oblivion made it necessary to veil all reference to this in general terms in no way diminished the strength of the prejudice against Socrates on this account. Among those of his associates who had proved enemies of the state none bore a heavier share of guilt than Alcibiades, and, as far as he is concerned, Plato supplements in the *Symposium* the defence of Socrates against the charge of 'corrupting the young' which he has already elaborated in the *Apology* and elsewhere. So too the anecdotes of Potidae and Delium serve a double purpose, revealing Socrates as patriotic citizen as well as true philosopher; there is indeed no end to the implications which may be traced in almost every line of Alcibiades' apparently unmethodical and extempore effusion.

One final point remains. Although, as has been said, the

views which Socrates expresses as the teaching of Diotima cannot be attributed to the historical Socrates, we need not hesitate to accept as a veracious portrait the picture presented to us by Alcibiades. The *Symposium* is a companion piece to the *Phaedo*; it represents Socrates in life as the *Phaedo* represents him in the hour of death, and in both dialogues historical fact is accompanied by a philosophical theory which cannot have been held by Socrates himself. In this matter the *Phaedo* is likely to offend the sensibilities of a modern reader even more than the *Symposium*, because it may seem to violate the sanctity of the hero's last moments; but in considering both we have to remember that however far Plato travelled beyond his master he never ceased to regard his own system as having been implicit in the methods and conclusions of Socrates – who remained for him, as he is here represented, the pattern of what human nature can be at its highest, the true philosopher in love.

THE SYMPOSIUM

•

CHARACTERS
OF THE DIALOGUE

APOLLODORUS, and an unnamed FRIEND to whom he narrates at second-hand the conversation of the following, which has been reported to him by ARISTODEMUS, a disciple of Socrates

AGATHON, a tragic poet, at whose house the party takes place

SOCRATES

ARISTODEMUS

PHAEDRUS, a hypochondriac literary man

PAUSANIAS, Agathon's lover } guests

ERYXIMACHUS, a doctor

ARISTOPHANES, the comic poet

ALCIBIADES, brilliant, dissolute, and notorious, now at the zenith of his power in Athens.

THE SYMPOSIUM

APOLLODORUS. I think I may say that I have already rehearsed the scene which you ask me to describe. The day before yesterday, as I was going up to town from my home at Phalerum, an acquaintance of mine caught sight of my back and shouted after me in a mock-official tone:

'Hi, you, Apollodorus of Phalerum, wait for me, can't you?'

I stood still and let him catch me up.

'I've just been looking for you, Apollodorus,' he said; 'I want to know what happened at that party of Agathon's with Socrates and Alcibiades and the others, and what was said on the subject of love. I've already had it from one person, who was told by Phoenix the son of Philip. He couldn't give me any clear account, but he said that you knew about it too. So please tell me; Socrates is your friend, and no one has a better right to report his conversation than you. First of all, were you at the party yourself?'

'It certainly can't have been at all a clear account,' I answered, 'if you suppose that the party that you are asking about took place at all recently, or that I was there.'

'I certainly did suppose so.'

'How could you, my dear Glaucon? Don't you know

that it is many years since Agathon lived in Athens, whereas it isn't three years yet since I first began to associate with Socrates, and to make it my business to know what he says and does every day? Before that I led a perfectly haphazard existence, and though I thought that I was getting somewhere, I was in fact the most wretched creature imaginable – quite as wretched as you are now – and believed that the pursuit of wisdom was the last thing a man should devote himself to.'

'Don't make fun of me,' he answered; 'tell me when this party happened.'

'While we were still boys,' I said, 'in the year that Agathon won the prize with his first tragedy, on the day after he held the usual celebration with the members of his cast in honour of his victory.'

'Quite a long time ago then. Who described it to you? Socrates himself?'

'No, indeed,' said I; 'the same person as told Phoenix, a man called Aristodemus from Cydathenaeum, a little fellow who always went about barefoot. He was at the party because he was, I believe, one of Socrates' greatest admirers in those days. But I did ask Socrates about a few of the particulars that Aristodemus gave me, and he confirmed his account.'

'Then why are you keeping me on tenterhooks? Our walk to town is an admirable opportunity for conversation.'

As we walked on together, then, we talked about the subject, so that, as I said at the beginning, I am not unrehearsed, and if you too want to hear the story I suppose I must comply. As a matter of fact, quite apart from any idea of edification, I take an extraordinary pleasure in talking myself, and in hearing others talk, on philosophical topics; but any other type of conversation — and particularly the talk of you rich business men — fills me with distress on my own account and with pity for those of you who are with me, because you think that you are accomplishing something when in fact you are accomplishing nothing. You in your turn may perhaps think me an unfortunate creature, and you are probably right, but my feeling about you is a matter not of opinion, but knowledge.

FRIEND. You're always the same, Apollodorus, — you're always running down yourself and other people; as far as I can see you believe that, but for Socrates, everybody in the world is wretched, beginning with yourself. I don't know where exactly you got your nickname of fanatic, but you live up to it in your conversation, at any rate; you are in a perpetual passion with everybody, yourself included, except Socrates.

APOLLODORUS. My dear friend, is it so perfectly clear that in holding this opinion of myself and you I show fanaticism and eccentricity?

FRIEND. We won't argue about that now, Apollodorus. Just confine yourself to doing what we asked, and describe the course of the conversation.

APOLLODORUS. Well, it was like this, — but I'd better try to describe it all from the beginning just as Aristodemus described it to me. His story was as follows:

'I met Socrates fresh from the bath and with shoes on his feet, two circumstances most unusual with him, and asked him where he was going so finely got up. "To dinner with Agathon. I shirked his victory party yesterday from dislike of the crowd, but I promised that I would be there today. As for my finery, one must look one's best when one is going to visit a good-looking man." Then he added: "How do you feel about coming with me to dinner, although you haven't been asked?" I said that I was at his disposal. "Come on then," he said. "We'll give a new turn to the old saying 'To good men's parties good men flock unasked';[1] it needs only the smallest change. As a matter of fact Homer seems to have done actual violence to the proverb and not merely perverted it. His Agamemnon is a pre-eminently good soldier whereas Menelaus is a 'feeble fighter', and yet, when Agamemnon makes a sacrifice and entertains his friends, Menelaus is represented as coming unasked, though his host is far the better man." "I'm afraid," I said, "that Homer's description will fit me better than yours, Socrates, a nobody going unasked to a pundit's party. If you take me you must think out some excuse; I won't admit that I've come unasked; I shall say that you asked me." "Let us be going," he said; "two heads will be better than one at deciding what to say."

'After this conversation we went on. But Socrates abandoned himself to his own thoughts and fell behind, and when I waited for him told me to go on without him. When I reached Agathon's house the door was open, and I found myself in a very ridiculous position. A servant met me at the door, and ushered me into the room where the guests were at table and already on the point of beginning dinner. As soon as Agathon saw me he cried out: "You have come just in time to join us at dinner, Aristodemus. If your visit has any other object, put it off for the moment. I tried to find you yesterday to ask you, but couldn't see you anywhere. But why haven't you brought Socrates with you?" I turned round, but couldn't see Socrates anywhere. So I said that I had, as a matter of fact, come with Socrates, and that he had invited me to dinner. "Splendid," said Agathon. "But where is Socrates?" "He was following me just now; I can't think what has become of him." "Go and look," Agathon said to a servant, "and fetch Socrates in. And you, Aristodemus, sit down beside Eryximachus."

'The servant brought me water to wash before I sat down, and another servant came and said that Socrates had taken up his position in a neighbour's front porch, and was standing there, deaf to all the servant's entreaties to come in. "What an odd thing," said Agathon. "Go and call him again and don't take no for an answer." "No," I said, "let him alone. It's a way he has. He goes apart sometimes and stands still wherever he happens to be. He will come presently, I am sure; don't bother him, but let him be." "Well, if you think so," said Agathon. Then to the servants: "Serve the rest of us anyhow. You have complete liberty to serve what you please when there is no one to supervise you, a thing that I have never bothered to do. So on this occasion treat us as your guests, me as much as the others, and see that your service deserves our praise."

'After that we began dinner, and still Socrates did not come. Agathon several times wanted to send for him, but I would not let him. Finally he came, not really very late for him, and found us about half-way through dinner. Agathon, as it happened, was sitting by himself at the bottom table,[2] and cried out: "Come and sit here beside me, Socrates, and let me, by contact with you, enjoy the discovery which you made in the porch. You must obviously have found the answer to your problem and pinned it down; you wouldn't have desisted till you had." Socrates sat down and said: "It would be very nice, Agathon, if wisdom were like water, and flowed by contact out of a person who has more into one who has less, just as water can be made to pass through a thread of wool out of the fuller of two cups into the emptier. If that applies to wisdom, I value the privilege of sitting beside you very highly, for I have no doubt that you will fill me with an ample draught of the finest wisdom. Such wisdom as I possess is slight and has little more reality than a dream, but yours is brilliant and may shine brighter yet; you are still quite young, and look at the dazzling way it flashed out the day before yesterday before an audience of more than thirty thousand Greeks." "Enough of your sarcasm, Socrates," replied Agathon. "We'll settle our respective claims to wisdom a little later on, and Dionysus, the god of wine, shall judge between us; for the moment give your attention to your dinner."

'When Socrates had settled himself and had his dinner like the rest, we poured libations and sang a hymn to the god and performed all the customary ritual actions, and then betook ourselves to drinking.[3] At this point Pausanias began as follows: "Come now, sirs, what will be the least rigorous rule to make about drinking? I don't mind telling you that yesterday's bout has left me in a very poor way, and I need a respite. I expect that most of you do too – you were there yesterday. So let us discuss what would be the least rigorous rule to make." "You are quite right, Pausanias," said Aristophanes, "to suggest that we should let ourselves off lightly. I am one of those who were pretty well soaked yesterday." "I entirely agree," said Eryximachus, the son of Acumenus, when he heard these remarks, "but there is still one person whose opinion I should like to have. How strong are you feeling, Agathon?" "Very weak," replied Agathon, "very weak indeed." "What a godsend for us," said Eryximachus, "I mean for me and Aristodemus and Phaedrus and our other friends, that you who have the strongest heads among us have given in; we are never able to compete. I don't count Socrates; both methods suit him equally well, and he will be content whichever we adopt. But since there appears to be no one here at all eager for serious drinking, perhaps you will bear with me if I tell you the truth about getting drunk. My medical experience has convinced me that drunkenness is bad for people; and I should be very unwilling either to drink at all deeply myself or to recommend such a course to anyone else, especially anyone who still had a hang-over from the previous day." Here Phaedrus from Myrrhinus interposed and said: "Well, I have always been in the habit of taking your advice, especially in medical matters, and the others will do so too on this occasion, if they are wise." After this everyone agreed that the present party should not be pushed to the point of drunkenness, but that we should drink merely as we felt inclined.

' "Since, then, we have come to this decision," said

Eryximachus, "that each man shall drink merely as much as he chooses, and that there shall be no compulsion, I propose in addition that we should send away the flute-girl who has just come in – let her play to herself or, if she likes, to the women of the household – and entertain ourselves today with conversation. If you ask on what subject, I have a proposal to make about that too, if you care to hear it." Everybody said that they would like to hear and bade him proceed. "I will begin," he said, "in the manner of Melanippe in Euripides; *not mine the tale* that I am going to tell; it belongs to our friend Phaedrus. He is always saying indignantly to me: 'Isn't it a shame, Eryximachus, that while certain of the other gods have hymns and songs of praise addressed to them by the poets, not one in all the multitude of poets has ever composed a single panegyric of so ancient and mighty a god as Love? Or take our good professional educators,[4] the excellent Prodicus for example; they write prose eulogies of Heracles and others – that is perhaps not so surprising – but I once came across a book by a learned man in which the usefulness of salt was made the subject of a wonderful panegyric, and you could find plenty of other things that have received similar treatment; but the pity is that, while such subjects as these have had immense pains bestowed on them, nobody to this day has had the courage to praise Love in such terms as he deserves. So completely has this mighty god been neglected.' I think that Phaedrus is right; I should therefore like to gratify him by offering him a contribution, and I also feel that it would be highly suitable for us who are present on this occasion to honour the god. If you agree, we shall not need anything beyond conversation to occupy us; my proposal is that each of us, going from left to right, should make the best speech he can in praise of love, and that Phaedrus should begin, since he is not only sitting furthest to the left but is also the begetter of the idea."

' "Nobody will vote against your proposal, Eryximachus," said Socrates. "I certainly shall not, for I declare that love is the only subject that I understand, nor will Agathon and Pausanias, I am sure, nor yet Aristophanes, whose entire business lies with Dionysus and Aphrodite, nor anyone else that I see here. It will, of course, be unfair to those of us who occupy the last places, but if fine performances by earlier speakers exhaust the subject, we shan't mind. Let Phaedrus begin and speak in praise of love, and good luck to him." '

All the rest concurred in what Socrates said, and called on Phaedrus to begin. Aristodemus did not recollect precisely everything that each speaker said, and I do not recollect everything that Aristodemus told me, but I will tell you the most important points in each of the speeches that seemed to me worth remembering.

As I have said, Aristodemus told me that Phaedrus began, choosing as his starting-point the statement that Love is a great god, revered among men and gods for many reasons, and not least on account of his birth.

'That the god should be one of the most ancient of all beings is a title to honour,' he said, 'and as evidence of this I can point to the fact that Love has no parents, and that parents are never ascribed to him by any writer either of prose or verse. Hesiod tells us that Chaos first came into existence,

> but next
> Broad-breasted Earth, on whose foundation firm
> Creation stands, and Love.

Acusilaus[5] agrees with Hesiod in saying that after Chaos these two, Earth and Love, came into being. And Parmenides in speaking of creation says

> First among all the gods she invented Love.[6]

So you see that there is widespread agreement about the extreme antiquity of Love.

'Now, as Love is the oldest of the gods, so also he confers upon us the greatest benefits, for I would maintain that there can be no greater benefit for a boy than to have a worthy lover from his earliest youth, nor for a lover than to have a worthy object for his affection. The principle which ought to guide the whole life of those who intend to live nobly cannot be implanted either by family or by position or by wealth or by anything else so effectively as by love. What principle? you ask. I mean the principle which inspires shame at what is disgraceful and ambition for what is noble; without these feelings neither a state nor an individual can accomplish anything great or fine. Suppose a lover to be detected in the performance of some dishonourable action or in failing through cowardice to defend himself when dishonour is inflicted upon him by another; I assert that there is no one, neither his father nor his friends nor anyone else, whose observation would cause him so much pain in such circumstances as his beloved's.

And conversely we see with regard to the beloved that he is peculiarly sensitive to dishonour in the presence of his lovers. If then one could contrive that a state or an army should entirely consist of lovers and loved,[7] it would be impossible for it to have a better organization than that which it would then enjoy through their avoidance of all dishonour and their mutual emulation; moreover, a handful of such men, fighting side by side, would defeat practically the whole world. A lover would rather be seen by all his comrades leaving his post or throwing away his arms than by his beloved; rather than that, he would prefer a thousand times to die. And if it were a question of deserting his beloved or not standing by him in danger, no one is so base as not to be inspired on such an occasion by Love himself with a spirit which would make him the equal of men with the best natural endowment of courage. In short, when Homer spoke of God "breathing might" into some of the heroes, he described exactly the effect which Love, of his very nature, produces in men who are in love.

'Moreover, only lovers will sacrifice their lives for another; this is true of women as well as men. In speaking to Greeks I need no example to support this assertion beyond that provided by Pelias' daughter Alcestis.[8] She was the only person who was willing to die for her husband, though he had a father and mother living, and the affection which love inspired in her was so surpassing that it made them appear mere strangers to their son, and his kindred in nothing but name. Her heroism in making this sacrifice appeared so noble in the eyes not only of men but of the gods, that they conferred upon

43

her a privilege which has been granted to very few among the many performers of noble deeds. In admiration of her behaviour they released her soul from Hades; so highly do even the gods honour the active courage which belongs to love. But Orpheus[9] the son of Oeagrus they sent away from Hades disappointed of the wife he had come to fetch – what they showed him was a mere ghost and they did not surrender her real person – because he seemed to lack spirit, as is only natural in a musician; he had not the courage to die for love like Alcestis, but contrived to enter Hades alive. For this they punished him and caused him to meet his death at the hands of women; whereas they honoured Achilles the son of Thetis and despatched him to the Islands of the Blest,[10] because he, when he learnt from his mother that he would die if he killed Hector, but that if he did not kill him he would reach home and die at a good old age, made the heroic choice to go to the rescue of his lover Patroclus and to avenge him, though this involved dying after him as well as for him. He thus earned the extreme admiration of the gods, who treated him with special distinction for showing in this way how highly he valued his lover.

'Aeschylus, by the way, is quite wrong when he says that Achilles was the lover of Patroclus. Achilles was the more beautiful of the two – indeed he was the most beautiful of all the heroes – and he was still beardless and according to Homer much younger than Patroclus. The truth is that, while the gods greatly honour the courage of a lover, they admire even more and reward more richly affection shown towards a lover by the beloved, because a lover is possessed and thus comes nearer than the beloved to being divine.[11] That is why they honoured Achilles more highly than Alcestis and sent him to the Islands of the Blest.

'I maintain then that Love is not only the oldest and most honourable of the gods, but also the most powerful to assist men in the acquisition of merit and happiness, both here and hereafter.'

This or something like it, according to Aristodemus, was the speech of Phaedrus. It was followed by several others which he did not quite remember, so he passed them by and went on to report the speech of Pausanias, which was as follows.

'I cannot agree, Phaedrus, with the condition laid down for our speeches, that they should be a simple and unqualified panegyric of Love. If Love had a single nature, it would be all very well, but not as it is, since Love is not single; and that being so the better course would be to declare in advance which Love it is that we have to praise. I will try to put the matter right by determining first of all which Love ought to be our subject, before going on to praise him in such terms as he deserves. We all know that Aphrodite is inseparably linked with Love. If there were a single Aphrodite there would be a single Love, but as there are two Aphrodites, it follows that there must be two Loves as well. Now what are the two Aphrodites? One is the elder and is the daughter of Uranus and had no mother; her we call Heavenly Aphrodite. The other is younger, the child of Zeus and Dione, and is called Common Aphrodite.[12] It follows that the Love which is the partner of the latter should be called Common Love and the other Heavenly Love. Of course, I am not denying that we ought to praise all the gods, but our present business is to discover what are the respective characters of these two Loves. Now the truth about every activity is that in itself it is neither good nor bad. Take the activities in which we are at present engaged, drinking and singing and conversation; none of these is good in itself; they derive their character from the way in which they are used. If it is well and rightly used, an activity becomes good, if wrongly, bad. So with the activity of love and Love himself. It is not Love absolutely that is good or praiseworthy, but only that Love which impels men to love aright.

'There can be no doubt of the common nature of the Love which goes with Common Aphrodite; it is quite random in the effects which it produces, and it is this love which the baser sort of men feel. Its marks are, first, that it is directed towards women quite as much as young men; second, that in either case it is physical rather than spiritual; third, that it prefers that its objects should be as unintelligent as possible, because its only aim is the satisfaction of its desires, and it takes no account of the manner in which this is achieved. That is why its effect is purely a matter of chance, and quite as often bad as good. In all this it partakes of the nature of its corresponding goddess, who is far younger than her heavenly counterpart, and who owes her birth to the conjunction of male and female. But the Heavenly Aphrodite to whom the other Love belongs for one thing has no female strain in her, but springs entirely

from the male,[13] and for another is older and consequently free from wantonness. Hence those who are
inspired by this Love are attracted towards the male sex,
and value it as being naturally the stronger and more in-
telligent. Besides, even among the lovers of their own
sex one can distinguish those whose motives are entirely
dictated by this second Love; they do not fall in love
with mere boys, but wait until they reach the age at
which they begin to show some intelligence, that is to
say, until they are near growing a beard. By choosing
that moment in the life of their favourite to fall in love
they show, if I am not mistaken, that their intention is
to form a lasting attachment and a partnership for life;
they are not the kind who take advantage of the ignorance of a boy to deceive him, and then are off with a
jeer in pursuit of some fresh darling. If men were for-
bidden by law, as they should be, to form connexions
with young boys, they would be saved from laying out
immense pains for a quite uncertain return; nothing is
more unpredictable than whether a young boy will turn
out spiritually and physically perfect or the reverse. As
things are, good men impose this rule voluntarily on
themselves, and it would be a good thing if a similar
restriction were laid upon the common sort of lovers; it
would be a correlative of the attempt which we already
make to forbid them to form connexions with free-
born women. It is men like these who bring love into
disrepute, and encourage some people to say that it is
disgraceful to yield to a lover; it is their lack of dis-
cretion and self-control that gives rise to such stric-
tures, for there is no action whatever that deserves to

be reprobated if it is performed in a decent and regular way.

'If we go on to consider what men's code of behaviour prescribes in the matter of love, we shall find that, whereas in other cities principles are laid down in black and white and are thus easily comprehensible, ours are more complicated. In Elis and Boeotia and Sparta and wherever men are unready of speech the code states quite simply that it is good to gratify a lover, and no one, young or old, would say that it is disgraceful.[14] The fact is, I imagine, that being poor speakers they wish to save themselves the trouble of having to win young men's favours by persuasive speeches. In many parts of Ionia, on the other hand, and elsewhere under Persian rule, the state of affairs is quite the reverse. The reason why such love, together with love of intellectual and physical achievement, is condemned by the Persians is to be found in the absolute nature of their empire; it does not suit the interest of the government that a generous spirit and strong friendships and attachments should spring up among their subjects, and these are effects which love has an especial tendency to produce. The truth of this was actually experienced by our tyrants at Athens; it was the love of Aristogiton and the strong affection of Harmodius which destroyed their power.[15] We may conclude then that where such love has been condemned it is the poor character of the people, greed for power in the rulers and cowardice in the subjects, which lies behind such a condemnation, but that where it has been thought to be unreservedly good this is due to mental indolence in the legislators.

'Our institutions are far nobler than these, but, as I
said, are not easily comprehensible. On the one hand, a
love which courts no concealment is reckoned among us
nobler than a love which shuns observation, and the love
of those who are most eminent by birth or merit, even
though they may be inferior in looks, is held in the
highest esteem. Besides this, the universal encourage-
ment which a lover receives is evidence that no stigma
attaches to him; success in a love-affair is glorious, and
it is only failure that is disgraceful, and we do not merely
tolerate, we even praise the most extraordinary behaviour in a lover in pursuit of his beloved, behaviour
which would meet with the severest condemnation if it
were practised for any other end. If a man, for example,
with the object of obtaining a present of money or a
public post or some other position of power, brought
himself to behave as a lover behaves towards his
favourite, begging and praying for the fulfilment of his
requests, making solemn promises, camping on doorsteps, and voluntarily submitting to a slavery such as no
slave ever knew, he would be restrained from such conduct by enemies and friends alike; the former would
abuse him for his servility and lack of spirit, and the
latter would give him good advice and blush for him.
But in a lover such actions as these constitute an added
charm, and no disgrace attends their performance by
our standards, because we recognize that the business
which he is about is supremely noble. What is strangest
of all is the popular conviction that a lover, and none but
a lover, can forswear himself with impunity – a lover's
vow, they say, is no vow at all. So we see that according

to our way of thinking a lover is allowed the utmost licence by both God and man, and the natural conclusion would be that in this country it is a very fine thing both to be in love and to show complaisance towards one's lovers. But when we reflect that the boys who inspire this passion are placed by their fathers in the charge of tutors, with injunctions not to allow them to hold any communication with their lovers, and that a boy who is involved in such communication is teased by his contemporaries and friends, and that their elders make no attempt to stop this teasing and do not condemn it, we are led to the opposite conclusion, and infer that such love is reckoned among us to be highly disgraceful.

'The truth of the matter I believe to be this. There is, as I stated at first, no absolute right and wrong in love, but everything depends upon the circumstances; to yield to a bad man in a bad way is wrong, but to yield to a worthy man in a right way is right. The bad man is the common or vulgar lover, who is in love with the body rather than the soul; he is not constant because what he loves is not constant; as soon as the flower of physical beauty, which is what he loves, begins to fade, he is gone "even as a dream", and all his professions and promises are as nothing. But the lover of a noble nature remains its lover for life, because the thing to which he cleaves is constant. The object of our custom then is to subject lovers to a thorough test; it encourages the lover to pursue and the beloved to flee, in order that the right kind of lover may in the end be gratified and the wrong kind eluded; it sets up a kind of competition to determine to which kind lover and beloved respectively belong. This is the motive which lies behind our general feeling that two things are discreditable, first, to give in quickly to a lover – time, which is the best test of most things, must be allowed to elapse – and second, to give in on account of his wealth or power, either because one is frightened and cannot hold out under the hardships which he inflicts, or because one cannot resist the material and political advantages which he confers; none of these things is stable or constant, quite apart from the fact that no noble friendship can be founded upon them.

'According to our principles there is only one way in which a lover can honourably enjoy the possession of his beloved. We hold that, just as a lover may submit to any form of servitude to his beloved without shameful servility, so there is one, and only one, other form of voluntary servitude which brings with it no dishonour, and that is servitude which has for its object the acquisition of excellence. If a person likes to place himself at the disposal of another because he believes that in this way he can improve himself in some department of knowledge, or in some other excellent quality, such a voluntary submission involves by our standards no taint of disgrace or servility. If the connexion between a lover and his beloved is to be honourable, both the principles which I have enunciated must be found in combination, that which deals with the behaviour of a lover of boys, and that which is concerned with the desire for knowledge or other forms of excellence. When a lover and his favourite come together, each in conformity with the principle which is appropriate to him, which is for the former that he is justified in performing any service whatever in return for the favours of his beloved, and for the latter that he is justified in any act of compliance to one who can make him wise and good, and when the lover is able to contribute towards wisdom and excellence, and the beloved is anxious to improve his education and knowledge in general, then and then only, when these two principles coincide, and in no other circumstances is it honourable for a boy to yield to his lover. In these circumstances too there is no disgrace in being deceived, whereas in all others a boy is disgraced whether he is deceived or not. Suppose that a boy grants favours to a lover believing him to be rich, and is then disappointed of his hope of gain by the lover turning out to be poor; the boy is disgraced nonetheless, because he has shown himself to be the sort of person who would do any service to anybody for money. But by the same reasoning if a boy grants favours to a lover believing that he is a good man and that he himself will be improved by association with him, and is disappointed because the lover turns out to be bad and devoid of merit, it does him credit to have been so deceived; he also has revealed his true nature, which is to be willing to do anything for anybody in order to attain excellence and improve himself, and nothing can be more honourable than that. So we conclude that it is in all cases honourable to comply with a lover to attain excellence. This is the Heavenly Love which is associated with the Heavenly Goddess, and which is valuable both to states and to individuals because it entails upon both lover and beloved self-discipline for the attainment of excellence. All other forms of love belong to the other Goddess, the Common Aphrodite. This is the best contribution that I can improvise for you, Phaedrus, on the subject of love.'

When Pausanias came to a pause (that is the sort of play upon words which I have picked up from the experts), it was Aristophanes' turn to speak, according to Aristodemus, but, whether from surfeit or from some other cause, he was suffering from a hiccup which prevented him speaking. So he said to Eryximachus the doctor, who was sitting next below him:

'You must either cure my hiccup, Eryximachus, or speak instead of me until it stops.'

'I will do both,' replied Eryximachus. 'I will take your turn and you shall take mine when you are better. As for the hiccup, hold your breath for a good time while I am speaking. If that doesn't cure it, gargle with water. If the hiccup is too violent even for that, get something to tickle your nose with, and sneeze. One or two sneezes, and it will stop, however violent.'

'Very well, I will do that,' said Aristophanes, 'and do you in the meantime get on with your speech.'

Eryximachus then spoke as follows:

'Pausanias, after an admirable beginning, has not brought his argument to an adequate conclusion; I think therefore that it is incumbent on me to try to put the finishing touches to it. He was quite right, in my opinion, in the distinction which he drew between the two kinds of love, but my professional experience as a doctor has shown me that love does not operate only in men's souls and has not only beautiful boys as its object, but that it has many other objects and other spheres of action, the bodies of all animals, for example, and plants which grow in the earth, and practically all existing things; in fact Love is a great and wonderful god whose influence extends everywhere, and embraces the worlds of gods and men alike.

'I will begin with medicine, to show my respect for the craft. Our physical constitution involves a double love; a healthy body is admittedly different from a diseased body and unlike it. Now the objects of the desire and love felt by unlike things are themselves unlike; so the love which exists in a healthy body is different from the love which exists in a diseased body. The fact is that in dealing with men's bodies we find an analogy with what Pausanias said a moment ago; just as honour and dishonour consist in yielding to the desires of virtuous and vicious men respectively, so it is the duty of a good practitioner to gratify the sound and healthy parts of the body and to thwart the unsound and diseased, and this is the business of what we call medicine, which is, in a word, the knowledge of the principles of love at work in the body in regard to repletion and evacuation. The most skilful doctor is the doctor who can distinguish between noble and base loves in this sphere, and the man who can cause a body to change the latter for the former, and can implant love in a body which lacks but needs it, and remove it where it already exists, will be a good practitioner. He must be able to bring elements in the body which are most hostile to one another into mutual affection and love; such hostile elements are the opposites hot and cold, wet and dry, and the like; it was by knowing how to create love and harmony between these that our forefather Asclepius, as our poets here say and as I believe, founded our craft.[16]

'Medicine then, I repeat, is entirely under the control of this god; and so are the arts of physical culture and of farming. That the same is true of music is plain to anyone who gives the smallest attention to the subject, and this is presumably what Heraclitus means to say, though he is not very happy in his choice of words, when he speaks of a unity which agrees with itself by being at variance, as in the stringing of a bow or a lyre. It is, of course, quite illogical to speak of a concord being in discord, or of its consisting of factors which are still in discord at the time when they compose it, but probably what he meant to say was that the art of music produces a harmony out of factors which are first in discord but subsequently in concord, namely treble and bass notes.[17] There can be no accord of treble and bass as long as they are in discord, for concord is consonance, and consonance is a kind of agreement, and it is impossible for there to be agreement between discordant elements as long as they are in discord; but it is possible to harmonize what is in discord and disagreement, just as rhythm results from the combination of fast and slow, factors which are originally discordant but subsequently in agreement. Music, by implanting mutual love and sympathy, causes agreement between these elements, just as medicine does in its different sphere, and music in its turn may be called a knowledge of the principles of love in the realm of harmony and rhythm. In the actual constitution of a harmony there is no difficulty in perceiving the principle of love at work, and the question of the double nature of love does not so far arise; but when one has to deal with the effect upon human beings of rhythm and harmony, either in their creation by the process known as composition, or in the right use of melodies and verse-forms in what is called education, difficulties occur which demand a skilful artist. We come back to our old notion that it is the love felt by virtuous men which should be gratified and preserved, with the object of making those more virtuous who are as yet less so. This is the noble, the heavenly love, which is associated with the heavenly muse, Urania. But there is also a vulgar or common love, associated with Polyhymnia, and anyone who employs this must exercise great caution in his choice of people upon whom to employ it, so as to cull the pleasure which it affords without implanting any taint of debauchery.[18] Similarly in my profession it is a matter of no little skill to make the right use of men's appetite for rich food, so that they may enjoy the pleasure it brings without incurring disease. Both kinds of love then must be the object of our vigilant care, in music and in medicine and in all other matters, both human and divine, for both are to be found in them all.

'Moreover, the seasons of the year are so ordained as to exhibit the operation of both kinds of love. When the elements of which I spoke before, hot and cold and dry and wet, are bound together in love which is orderly, and combined harmoniously in due proportions, man and the other animals and plants thrive and are healthy and take no harm. But when inordinate love gets the upper hand in the matter of the seasons, it causes widespread destruction and injury; from this, epidemics and many other various ailments are apt to spring; frost, hail, and blight are the result of the mutual disorderly aggression of these elements under the influence of love. The effects of that influence upon the courses of the stars and the seasons of the year are the object of the department of knowledge which is called astronomy.

'Again, all sacrifices and acts which fall within the province of divination (and these comprise the whole subject of the mutual relations of gods and men) are entirely directed to the preservation or the cure of love. Sin of all kinds is the result of gratifying and honouring and exalting in one's every action the vicious instead of the virtuous love, whether the persons affected by such behaviour be one's parents, either living or dead, or the gods. In these matters it is the function of divination to oversee the two kinds of love, and to effect a cure where it is needed; divination is the craft which establishes good-will between gods and men, because it understands the principles of love which, in human life, issue in virtuous and god-fearing behaviour.

'So then love in general exercises a multifarious and great, or, to speak more accurately, an omnipotent sway, but it is the love whose object is good and whose fulfilment is attended by sobriety and virtue, whether in heaven or earth, that possesses the greater power, and is the author of all our happiness, and makes it possible for us to live in harmony and concord with our fellow-creatures and with the gods, our masters. It may be that in my panegyric of love I have omitted several points, but, if so, it has been unwittingly. If I *have* left anything out, it is for you, Aristophanes, to fill the gaps, unless you plan to take some other line in praising the god. Now is your time to speak, since your hiccup has stopped.'

So it came to Aristophanes' turn, who began, according to Aristodemus, as follows:

'Yes, it stopped, but not till I applied the sneezing treatment. I can't help wondering whether it is the virtuous love in my body which desires such noises and tickling sensations as a sneeze. At any rate, the hiccup stopped at once as soon as I applied your method.'

'My dear Aristophanes,' said Eryximachus, 'take care what you're about. If you preface what you have to say by making us laugh, you will force me to be on the watch for jokes in your speech, which might otherwise run its course in peace.'

'Quite right, Eryximachus,' replied Aristophanes, laughing. 'I take back what I said. As for what I am going to say, don't watch me too strictly, for my fear is, not that it may raise a smile – that would be all to the good and quite in accordance with the nature of my muse – but that it may be downright absurd.'

'Ah, you think that you can have your joke and escape the consequences, Aristophanes. But take care, and remember in making your speech that you will be called to account, and then perhaps, if I see fit, I may let you off.'

'Well, Eryximachus,' began Aristophanes, 'it is quite true that I intend to take a different line from you and Pausanias. Men seem to me to be utterly insensible of the power of Love; otherwise he would have had the largest temples and altars and the largest sacrifices. As it is, he has none of these things, though he deserves them most of all. For of all the gods he is the most friendly to man, and his helper and physician in those diseases whose cure constitutes the greatest happiness of the human race. I shall therefore try to initiate you into the secret of his power, and you in turn shall teach others.

'First of all, you must learn the constitution of man and the modifications which it has undergone, for originally it was different from what it is now. In the first place there were three sexes, not, as with us, two, male and female; the third partook of the nature of both the others and has vanished, though its name survives. The hermaphrodite was a distinct sex in form as well as in name, with the characteristics of both male and female, but now the name alone remains, and that solely as a term of abuse. Secondly, each human being was a rounded whole, with double back and flanks forming a complete circle; it had four hands and an equal number of legs, and two identically similar faces upon a circular neck, with one head common to both the faces, which were turned in opposite directions. It had four ears and two organs of generation and everything else to correspond. These people could walk upright like us in either direction, backwards or forwards, but when they wanted to run quickly they used all their eight limbs, and turned rapidly over and over in a circle, like tumblers who perform a cart-wheel and return to an upright position. The reason for the existence of three sexes and for their being of such a nature is that originally the male sprang from the sun and the female from the earth, while the sex which was both male and female came from the moon, which partakes of the nature of both sun and earth. Their circular shape and their hoop-like method of progression were both due to the fact that they were like their parents. Their strength and vigour made them very formidable, and their pride was overweening; they attacked the gods, and Homer's story of Ephialtes and Otus attempting to climb up to heaven and set upon the gods is related also of these beings.[19]

'So Zeus and the other gods debated what was to be done with them. For a long time they were at a loss, unable to bring themselves either to kill them by lightning, as they had the giants, and extinguish the race – thus depriving themselves for ever of the honours and sacrifice due from humanity – or to let them go on in their insolence. At last, after much painful thought, Zeus had an idea. "I think," he said, "that I have found a way by which we can allow the human race to continue to exist and also put an end to their wickedness by making them weaker. I will cut each of them in two; in this way they will be weaker, and at the same time more profitable to us by being more numerous. They shall walk upright upon two legs. If there is any sign of wantonness in them after that, and they will not keep quiet, I will bisect them again, and they shall hop on one leg." With these words he cut the members of the human race in half, just like fruit which is to be dried and preserved, or like eggs which are cut with a hair. As he bisected each, he bade Apollo turn round the face and the half-neck attached to it towards the cut side, so that the victim, having the evidence of bisection before his eyes, might behave better in future. He also bade him heal the wounds. So Apollo turned round the faces, and gathering together the skin, like a purse with draw-strings, on to what is now called the belly, he tied it tightly in the middle of the belly round a single aperture which men call the navel. He smoothed out the other wrinkles, which were numerous, and moulded the chest with a tool like those which cobblers use to smooth wrinkles in the leather on their last. But he left a few on the belly itself round the navel, to remind man of the state from which he had fallen.

'Man's original body having been thus cut in two, each half yearned for the half from which it had been severed. When they met they threw their arms round one another and embraced, in their longing to grow together again, and they perished of hunger and general neglect of their concerns, because they would not do anything apart. When one member of a pair died and the other was left, the latter sought after and embraced another partner, which might be the half either of a female whole (what is now called a woman) or a male. So they went on perishing till Zeus took pity on them, and hit upon a second plan. He moved their reproductive organs to the front: hitherto they had been placed on the outer side of their bodies, and the processes of be-getting and birth had been carried on not by the physical union of the sexes, but by emission on to the ground, as is the case with grasshoppers. By moving their genitals to the front, as they are now, Zeus made it possible for reproduction to take place by the intercourse of the male with the female. His object in making this change was twofold; if male coupled with female, children might be begotten and the race thus continued, but if male coupled with male, at any rate the desire for intercourse would be satisfied, and men set free from it to turn to other activities and to attend to the rest of the business of life. It is from this distant epoch, then, that we may date the innate love which human beings feel for one another, the love which restores us to our ancient state by attempting to weld two beings into one and to heal the wounds which humanity suffered.

'Each of us then is the mere broken tally of a man, the result of a bisection which has reduced us to a condition like that of flat fish, and each of us is perpetually in search of his corresponding tally. Those men who are halves of a being of the common sex, which was called, as I told you, hermaphrodite, are lovers of women, and most adulterers come from this class, as also do women who are mad about men and sexually promiscuous. Women who are halves of a female whole direct their affections towards women and pay little attention to men; Lesbians belong to this category. But those who are halves of a male whole pursue males, and being slices, so to speak, of the male, love men throughout their boyhood, and take pleasure in physical contact with men. Such boys and lads are the best of their generation, because they are the most manly. Some people say that they are shameless, but they are wrong. It is not shamelessness which inspires their behaviour, but high spirit and manliness and virility, which lead them to welcome the society of their own kind. A striking proof of this is that such boys alone, when they reach maturity, engage in public life. When they grow to be men, they become lovers of boys, and it requires the compulsion of convention to overcome their natural disinclination to marriage and procreation; they are quite content to live with one another unwed. In a word, such persons are devoted to lovers in boyhood and themselves lovers of boys in manhood, because they always cleave to what is akin to themselves.

'Whenever the lover of boys – or any other person for that matter – has the good fortune to encounter his own actual other half, affection and kinship and love combined inspire in him an emotion which is quite overwhelming, and such a pair practically refuse ever to be separated even for a moment. It is people like these who form lifelong partnerships, although they would find it difficult to say what they hope to gain from one another's society. No one can suppose that it is mere physical enjoyment which causes the one to take such intense delight in the company of the other. It is clear that the soul of each has some other longing which it cannot express, but can only surmise and obscurely hint at. Suppose Hephaestus with his tools were to visit them as they lie together, and stand over them and ask: "What is it, mortals, that you hope to gain from one another?" Suppose too that when they could not answer he repeated his question in these terms: "Is the object of your desire to be always together as much as possible, and never to be separated from one another day or night? If that is what you want, I am ready to melt and weld you together, so that, instead of two, you shall be one flesh; as long as you live you shall live a common life, and when you die, you shall suffer a common death, and be still one, not two, even in the next world. Would such a fate as this content you, and satisfy your longings?" We know what their answer would be; no one would refuse the offer; it would be plain that this is what everybody wants, and everybody would regard it as the precise expression of the desire which he had long felt but had been unable to formulate, that he should melt into his beloved, and that henceforth they should be one being instead of two. The reason is that this was our primitive condition when we were wholes, and love is simply the name for the desire and pursuit of the whole. Originally, as I say, we were whole beings, before our wickedness caused us to be split by Zeus, as the Arcadians have been split apart by the Spartans.[20] We have reason to fear that if we do not behave ourselves in the sight of heaven, we may be split in two again, like dice which are bisected for tallies, and go about like the people represented in profile on tombstones, sawn in two vertically down the line of our noses. That is why we ought to exhort everyone to conduct himself reverently towards the gods; we shall thus escape a worse fate, and even win the blessings which Love has in his power to bestow, if we take him for our guide and captain. Let no man set himself in opposition to Love – which is the same thing as incurring the hatred of the gods – for if we are his friends and make our peace with him, we shall succeed, as few at present succeed, in finding the person to love who in the strictest sense belongs to us. I know that Eryximachus is anxious to make fun of my speech, but he is not to suppose that in saying this I am pointing at Pausanias and Agathon. They may, no doubt, belong to this class, for they are both unquestionably halves of male wholes, but I am speaking of men and women in general when I say that the way to happiness for our race lies in fulfilling the behests of Love, and in each finding for himself the mate who properly belongs to him; in a word, in returning to our original condition. If that condition was the best, it follows that it is best for us to come as near to it as our present circumstances allow; and the way to do that is to find a sympathetic and congenial object for our affections.

'If we are to praise the god who confers this benefit upon us, it is to Love that our praises should be addressed. It is Love who is the author of our well-being in this present life, by leading us towards what is akin to us, and it is Love who gives us a sure hope that, if we conduct ourselves well in the sight of heaven, he will hereafter make us blessed and happy by restoring us to our former state and healing our wounds.

'There is my speech about Love, Eryximachus, and you will see that it is of quite a different type from yours. Remember my request, and don't make fun of it, but let us hear what each of the others has to say. I should have said "each of the other two", for only Agathon and Socrates are left.'

'Well, I will do as you ask,' said Eryximachus; 'I won't deny that your speech gave me very considerable pleasure. Indeed, if I didn't know that Socrates and Agathon were authorities on the subject of love, I should be afraid that they might find the subject exhausted by the various speeches already made. But as it is I have complete confidence in them.'

'It is all very well for you, Eryximachus,' said Socrates. 'You have just given a fine performance yourself. But if you were in my present position, or rather in the position which I shall be in shortly, when Agathon too has distinguished himself, you would be in a panic and at your wit's end, as I am now.'

'You're trying to put a spell on me with your flattery, Socrates,' Agathon said. 'You want to upset me by making me think that the audience has formed great expectations of my eloquence.'

'I should be forgetful indeed, my dear Agathon, if, after seeing your courage and high spirit when you appeared upon the platform with the actors just before the production of your play, and faced a crowded audience without the least sign of embarrassment, I now supposed that you were likely to be upset by a handful of people like us.'

'But you surely don't suppose, Socrates, that I am so stage-struck as not to know that to a man of sense a handful of wise men is more formidable than a crowd of fools?'

'I should be very wrong if I entertained any opinion derogatory to your intelligence, Agathon. Of course, I know that you pay more attention to those whom you consider wise than to ordinary people; only I am afraid that we do not belong to the former class. We were in the theatre, you know, and part of the audience of ordinary people. But if you were to meet really wise men, you would probably feel shame before them if you were conscious of doing something discreditable, wouldn't you?'

'Of course I should.'

'But you wouldn't feel shame before ordinary people in the same circumstances?'

Here Phaedrus interposed and said:

'Don't answer Socrates, my dear Agathon. Provided that he has somebody to talk to, particularly if that somebody is good-looking, he won't care in the least what happens to our project. I'm very fond myself of hearing Socrates talk, but my present duty is to watch over the interest of Love, and receive a contribution of praise from each one of you.'

'Quite right, Phaedrus,' said Agathon, 'and there's nothing to prevent me from making my speech. There will be plenty of other opportunities of conversing with Socrates.

'My intention is first to state the principles which should guide me in my speech, and then to make the speech itself. All the previous speakers seem to me to have dwelt upon the happiness of humanity in being endowed by the god with such blessings, rather than upon the praise of the god himself; no one has said what sort of being he is who has conferred these gifts. The only right way of composing any panegyric is to set out the nature of the subject of the panegyric as well as the effects of which that subject is the cause; that is the way in which we ought to praise Love, describing first his nature and afterwards the gifts which he bestows.

'I maintain then that of all the happy company of

the gods Love (if I may say so without incurring the jealousy of heaven) is the most happy, in so far as he is the fairest and best. That he is the fairest may be established by the following considerations. First of all, Phaedrus, he is the youngest of the gods. He himself provides convincing evidence of the truth of what I say by fleeing before old age, which moves fast, as we know; at any rate it advances upon us faster than it should. It is the nature of Love to hate old age, and not to come even within long range of it. His whole life is passed in the company of the young, for there is truth in the old saying that like clings to like. Though I agree with Phaedrus in much else I cannot agree with him in this, that Love is of antediluvian antiquity. I maintain, on the contrary, that he is the youngest of the gods and always young, and that the ancient disturbances in heaven of which Hesiod and Parmenides tell are to be ascribed to the agency of Necessity and not of Love, if they happened at all. Mutilation, imprisonment, and many other like deeds of violence could never have occurred among the gods if Love had been there;[21] all would have been peace and friendship as it is now, and has been ever since Love assumed dominion over them.

'Love then is young, and besides being young he is sensitive to hardships. It would need a second Homer to describe how sensitive a god can be. Homer describes Infatuation as being not only divine but sensitive – or at any rate as having sensitive feet – when he says:

> Her feet are tender, and she never deigns
> To set them on the earth, but softly steps
> Upon the heads of men.

In my opinion he makes a very fine use of the idea of the goddess stepping on what is soft rather than hard to express her sensitive nature, and we may employ the same notion to illustrate the sensitiveness of Love. He does not step upon the earth, nor even upon men's heads, which after all are not so very soft; he lives and moves among the softest of all existing things; he has established his dwelling in the characters and souls of men. Not in all souls, for when he encounters a hard nature he departs; but he settles down wherever he finds one that is soft and yielding. Since, then, he clings not merely with his feet but with his whole being to what is the softest of the soft, it follows that he is extremely sensitive.

'Besides being very young and very sensitive he has a supple form. How, if he were stiff and unbending, could he wrap himself round everything, and be so stealthy in his first entrance into and in his departure from every soul? His very gracefulness, a quality in which he is universally admitted to be unsurpassed – for awkwardness is absolutely incompatible with Love – is evidence that he possesses a well-proportioned and supple shape. The beauty of his complexion is shown by his living among flowers; he never settles in any abode, be it a body or a soul or anything else, that is incapable of blooming or whose bloom has faded, but wherever he finds a spot that is flowery and fragrant, there he settles and abides.

'Though I have left many points untouched, these will suffice to demonstrate the beauty of the god. It remains to speak of his goodness. Here the most important point is that in his dealings with gods and men Love neither inflicts wrong upon either, nor suffers it from them. When he is passive it is not because violence is put upon him, for violence never touches Love, and when he is active he never employs it, for everyone willingly obeys Love in everything, and where there is mutual consent there is also what "the law, the sovereign ruler of society,"[22] proclaims to be right.

'In addition Love is richly endowed with self-control. Everyone admits that self-control is mastery over pleasures and desires, and that no pleasure is stronger than Love. If then all pleasures are weaker than Love, Love must be the master and they his subjects. So Love, being master over pleasures and desires, will be in a pre-eminent degree self-controlled.

'As for courage, Love "more than matches Ares",[23] the god of war. It is not Ares who captured Love, but Love who captured Ares, lover of Aphrodite to wit, according to tradition. Now the capturer is superior to the captive, and the capturer of the bravest of all other beings will necessarily be the bravest of all beings whatsoever.

'So much for the uprightness and self-control and courage of the god. His wisdom remains, and I must do my best to do justice to it. In the first place, if I may give my own craft the same precedence which Eryximachus gave to his, the god is so clever a poet that he can make others poets as well. At any rate, anyone whom Love touches becomes a poet, "although a stranger to the Muse before".[24] We should accept this as evidence that, broadly speaking, Love excels in every kind of artistic creation; how can anyone impart or teach to another an art which he does not possess or does not know? As for the creation of all kinds of living beings, no one will deny that this is an effect of the wisdom of love, by which all living things are born and grow. Finally, in the productions of craftsmanship, we know well that the man who has this god for his teacher turns out notable and famous, whereas the man who is untouched by Love remains obscure. It was under the guidance of desire and love that Apollo discovered the arts of archery and medicine and divination, so that he too may be called a pupil of Love, as the Muses are in literature, Hephaestus in blacksmith's work, Athene in weaving, and Zeus in the government of gods and men. Similarly, it was the birth of Love – love of beauty no doubt, since Love cannot attach himself to ugliness – which composed the troubles among the gods; before that, as I said at the beginning, tradition records that many frightful things happened in heaven, because Necessity was supreme. But as soon as this god was born, the love of beauty gave rise to all manner of blessings for gods and men alike.

'In my opinion, then, Phaedrus, Love is in the first place supreme in beauty and goodness himself, and in the second the cause of like qualities in others. Indeed, I feel inspired to express this idea in verse and to say that it is Love who creates

> Peace among men, and calm upon the sea,
> Rest for the winds from strife, and sleep in sorrow.

It is Love who empties us of the spirit of estrangement and fills us with the spirit of kinship; who makes possible such mutual intercourse as this; who presides over festivals, dances, sacrifices; who bestows good-humour and banishes surliness; whose gift is the gift of good-will and never of ill-will. He is easily entreated and of great kindness; contemplated by the wise, admired by the gods; coveted by men who possess him not, the treasure of those who are blessed by his possession; father of Daintiness, Delicacy, Voluptuousness, all Graces, Longing, and Desire; careful of the happiness of good men, careless of the fate of bad; in toil, in fear, in desire, in speech the best pilot, soldier, comrade, saviour; author of order in heaven and earth; loveliest and best of all leaders of song, whom it behoves every man to follow singing his praise, and bearing his part in that melody wherewith he casts a spell over the minds of all gods and all men.

'There is my speech, Phaedrus, a decent compound of playfulness and gravity, and let it be dedicated to the god as the best medley that I can contrive.'

When Agathon had finished speaking, all his hearers, according to Aristodemus, loudly proclaimed that the young poet had acquitted himself in a way worthy of himself and of the god. Socrates looked at Eryximachus, and said:

'Do you still think, son of Acumenus, that my fear was a groundless fear? Admit that I prophesied truly when I said that Agathon would give a wonderful performance, and that I should be at a loss.'

'I grant the prophetic nature of your remark about Agathon,' replied Eryximachus, 'but as for your being at a loss, I don't believe it.'

'My dear sir, how can I fail to be at a loss? How could anyone who had to speak after so splendid and varied an oration as that which we have just heard? The earlier part of it was not so remarkable as the rest, I know, but the beauty of the words and phrases in that passage at the end would have taken anyone's breath away. For my part, when I reflected that I should not be able to come anywhere near that standard of eloquence, I was on the point of running away for shame, and should very likely have done so if I had had anywhere to run to. Agathon's speech reminded me of Gorgias, and put me exactly in the position of the man in Homer; I was afraid that he would end by turning on my speech the Gorgon's head of Gorgias, that formidable orator, and thus reducing me to the speechlessness of a stone.[25]

'It was then that I realized how idiotic it was of me to agree to take part with you in praising Love, and to say that I was expert in love-matters, when, as it turned out, I was absolutely ignorant of the proper method of making a panegyric on any subject. I was stupid enough to suppose that the right thing was to speak the truth about the subject proposed for panegyric, whatever it might be, and that the truth would provide the material, as it were, out of which one selected the most favourable points and arranged them as artistically as possible. I was full of confidence in my ability to speak well, because I knew the true nature of Love. But now it appears that this is not the right way to set about praising anything, and that the proper method is to ascribe to the subject of the panegyric all the loftiest and loveliest qualities, whether it actually possesses them or not; if the ascription is false, it is after all a matter of no consequence. In fact, what was proposed to us was that each of us should give the appearance of praising Love rather than that we should actually do so. That is why, I imagine, you rake up stories of every kind and ascribe the credit of them to Love; that is why you depict his nature and the effects of his activity as you do. Your object is that in the eyes of those who do not know him – for such a description will never pass among experts – he should appear the loveliest and best of all beings, and your panegyric has a very fine and solemn sound. I, not knowing the proper method, agreed in my ignorance to contribute my share, but it was my tongue that gave the promise, not my mind.26 A fig for my promise, then. I'll no longer utter a panegyric, if it is to be after this fashion; I can't do it. I am quite willing to tell the truth in my own style, if you like; only I must not be regarded as competing with your speeches, or I shall be a laughing-stock. You had better consider, Phaedrus, whether you have any use for such a speech as I propose, a plain statement of the truth about Love, with only such diction and arrangement of phrases as may happen to occur to me on the spur of the moment.'

Phaedrus and the rest encouraged him to make a speech in the way which he himself thought right. So he continued:

'Allow me also, Phaedrus, to ask Agathon a few small questions, so that I may obtain his agreement before I begin my speech.'

'Certainly,' said Phaedrus, 'ask away.'

So Socrates began, according to Aristodemus, something like this.

'I was very much struck by your introductory passage, my dear Agathon, where you said that the right thing was first to describe the actual nature of the god, and afterwards to demonstrate the effects which he produces. I like that way of beginning very much. But I should be grateful if you would supplement your otherwise splendid and magnificent account of Love's nature by answering this question. Is the nature of Love such that he must be love of something, or can he exist absolutely without an object? I don't mean "Is Love love of a particular mother or father?" – to ask whether Love is love of a mother or father would be absurd – but I can make my point clear by analogy. If I were to take the single notion *Father* and ask "Does *Father* mean the father of someone or not?" you, if you wanted to give the right answer, would presumably reply that *Father* means the father of a son or a daughter, wouldn't you?'

'Certainly,' said Agathon.

'And similarly with *Mother*?'

'Agreed.'

'Let us go a little further, to make my meaning quite clear. The notion *Brother*, does that intrinsically imply brother of someone, or not?'

'Of course it does.'

'In fact, of a brother or sister?'

'Yes.'

'Very well. Now try to tell me whether Love means love of something, or whether there can be Love which is love of nothing.'

'Quite clearly, it means love of something.'

'Take a firm grasp of this point, then,' said Socrates, 'remembering also, though you may keep it to yourself for the moment, what it is that Love is love of. And now just tell me this: Does Love desire the thing that he is love of, or not?'

'Of course he does.'

'And does he desire and love the thing that he desires and loves when he is in possession of it or when he is not?'

'Probably when he is not.'

'If you reflect for a moment, you will see that it isn't merely probable but absolutely certain that one desires what one lacks, or rather that one does not desire what one does not lack. To me at any rate, Agathon, it seems as certain as anything can be. What do you think?'

'Yes, I think it is.'

'Good. Now would anybody wish to be big who was big, or strong who was strong?'

'It follows from my previous admission that this is impossible.'

'Because a man who possesses a quality cannot be in need of it?'

'Yes.'

'Suppose a man wanted to be strong who was strong, or swift-footed who was swift-footed. I labour the point in order to avoid any possibility of mistake, for one might perhaps suppose in these and all similar cases that people who are of a certain character or who possess certain qualities also desire the qualities which they possess. But if you consider the matter, Agathon, you will see that these people must inevitably possess these qualities at the present moment, whether they like it or not, and no one presumably would desire what is inevitable. No, if a man says: "I, who am healthy, or who am rich, nonetheless desire to be healthy or rich, as the case may be, and I desire the very qualities which I possess," we should reply: "My friend, what you, who are in possession of health and wealth and strength, really wish, is to have the possession of these qualities continued to you in the future, since at the present moment you possess them whether you wish it or not." Consider, then, whether when you say "I desire what I possess" you do not really mean "I wish that I may continue to possess in the future the things which I possess now." If it were put to him like this, he would agree, I think.'

'Yes,' said Agathon.

'But this is to be in love with a thing which is not yet in one's power or possession, namely the continuance and preservation of one's present blessings in the future.'

'Certainly.'

'Such a man, then, and everyone else who feels desire, desires what is not in his present power or possession, and desire and love have for their object things or qualities which a man does not at present possess but which he lacks.'

'Yes.'

'Come then,' said Socrates, 'let us sum up the points on which we have reached agreement. Are they not first that Love exists only in relation to some object, and second that that object must be something of which he is at present in want?'

'Yes.'

'Now recall also what it was that you declared in your speech to be the object of Love. I'll do it for you, if you like. You said, I think, that the troubles among the gods were composed by love of beauty, for there could not be such a thing as love of ugliness. Wasn't that it?'

'Yes.'

'Quite right, my dear friend, and if that is so, Love will be love of beauty, will he not, and not love of ugliness?'

Agathon agreed.

'Now we have agreed that Love is in love with what he lacks and does not possess.'

'Yes.'

'So after all Love lacks and does not possess beauty?'

'Inevitably.'

'Well then, would you call what lacks and in no way possesses beauty beautiful?'

'Certainly not.'

'Do you still think then that Love is beautiful, if this is so?'

'It looks, Socrates, as if I didn't know what I was talking about when I said that.'

'Still, it was a beautiful speech, Agathon. But there is just one more small point. Do you think that what is good is the same as what is beautiful?'

'I do.'

'Then, if Love lacks beauty, and what is good

coincides with what is beautiful, he also lacks goodness.'

'I can't find any way of withstanding you, Socrates. Let it be as you say.'

'Not at all, my dear Agathon. It is truth that you find it impossible to withstand; there is never the slightest difficulty in withstanding Socrates.

'But now I will leave you in peace, and try to give the account of Love which I once heard from a woman of Mantinea, called Diotima. She had other accomplishments as well – once, before the plague, when the Athenians had been sacrificing to avert it, she succeeded in postponing it for ten years – but what concerns us at present is that she was my instructress in the art of love. I will try, taking the conclusions on which Agathon and I reached agreement as my starting-point, to give the best consecutive account I can of what she told me. As you were so careful to point out to us, Agathon, one must elucidate the essential nature and characteristics of Love before describing his effects. The easiest thing will be to go through the same questions and answers as she did with me. I had used very much the same language to her as Agathon used to me, and had said that Love is a great god and must be reckoned beautiful, but she employed against me the arguments by which I demonstrated to Agathon that to my way of thinking Love is neither beautiful nor good. "What do you mean, Diotima?" I said. "Is Love ugly and bad?" "Don't say such things," she answered; "do you think that anything that is not beautiful is necessarily ugly?" "Of course I do." "And that anything that is not wisdom is ignorance?

Don't you know that there is a state of mind half-way between wisdom and ignorance?" "What do you mean?" "Having true convictions without being able to give reasons for them," she replied. "Surely you see that such a state of mind cannot be called understanding, because nothing irrational deserves the name; but it would be equally wrong to call it ignorance; how can one call a state of mind ignorance which hits upon the truth? The fact is that having true convictions is what I called it just now, a condition half-way between knowledge and ignorance." "I grant you that," said I. "Then do not maintain that what is not beautiful is ugly, and what is not good is bad. Do not suppose that because, on your own admission, Love is not good or beautiful, he must on that account be ugly and bad, but rather that he is something between the two." "And yet," I said, "everybody admits that he is a great god." "When you say everybody, do you mean those who don't know him, or do you include those who do?" "I mean absolutely everybody." She burst out laughing, and said: "Well, Socrates, I don't see how he can be admitted to be a great god by those who say that he isn't even a god at all." "Who are they?" I asked. "You are one of them and I'm another." "What can you mean?" "It's perfectly easy; you'd say, wouldn't you, that all gods are happy and beautiful? You wouldn't dare to suggest that any of the gods is not?" "Good heavens, no." "And by happy you mean in secure enjoyment of what is good and beautiful?" "Certainly." "But you have agreed that it is because he lacks what is good and beautiful that Love desires these very things." "Yes, I have." "But a being who has no share of the good and beautiful cannot be a god?" "Obviously not." "Very well then, you see that you are one of the people who believe that Love is not a god."

' "What can Love be then?" I said. "A mortal?" "Far from it." "Well, what?" "As in my previous examples, he is half-way between mortal and immortal." "What sort of being is he then, Diotima?" "He is a great spirit, Socrates; everything that is of the nature of a spirit is half-god and half-man." "And what is the function of such a being?" "To interpret and convey messages to the gods from men and to men from the gods, prayers and sacrifices from the one, and commands and rewards from the other. Being of an intermediate nature, a spirit bridges the gap between them, and prevents the universe from falling into two separate halves. Through this class of being come all divination and the supernatural skill of priests in sacrifices and rites and spells and every kind of magic and wizardry. God does not deal directly with man; it is by means of spirits that all the intercourse and communication of gods with men, both in waking life and in sleep, is carried on. A man who possesses skill in such matters is a spiritual man, whereas a man whose skill is confined to some trade or handicraft is an earthly creature. Spirits are many in number and of many kinds, and one of them is Love."

' "Who are his parents?" I asked. "That is rather a long story," she answered, "but I will tell you. On the day that Aphrodite was born the gods were feasting, among them Contrivance the son of Invention; and after dinner, seeing that a party was in progress, Poverty came to beg and stood at the door. Now Contrivance was drunk with nectar – wine, I may say, had not yet been discovered – and went out into the garden of Zeus, and was overcome by sleep. So Poverty, thinking to alleviate her wretched condition by bearing a child to Contrivance, lay with him and conceived Love. Since Love was begotten on Aphrodite's birthday, and since he has also an innate passion for the beautiful, and so for the beauty of Aphrodite herself, he became her follower and servant. Again, having Contrivance for his father and Poverty for his mother, he bears the following character. He is always poor, and, far from being sensitive and beautiful, as most people imagine, he is hard and weather-beaten, shoeless and homeless, always sleeping out for want of a bed, on the ground, on doorsteps, and in the street. So far he takes after his mother and lives in want. But, being also his father's son, he schemes to get for himself whatever is beautiful and good; he is bold and forward and strenuous, always devising tricks like a cunning huntsman; he yearns after knowledge and is full of resource and is a lover of wisdom all his life, a skilful magician, an alchemist, a true sophist. He is neither mortal nor immortal; but on one and the same day he will live and flourish (when things go well with him), and also meet his death; and then come to life again through the vigour that he inherits from his father. What he wins he always loses, and is neither rich nor poor, neither wise nor ignorant.

' "The truth of the matter is this. No god is a lover of wisdom or desires to be wise, for he is wise already, and the same is true of other wise persons, if there be any such. Nor on the other hand do the ignorant love wisdom and desire to be wise, for the tiresome thing about ignorance is precisely this, that a man who possesses neither beauty nor goodness nor intelligence is perfectly well satisfied with himself, and no one who does not believe that he lacks a thing desires what he does not believe that he lacks."

' "Who then," I said, "are the lovers of wisdom, if they are neither the wise nor the ignorant?" "A child could answer that question. Obviously they are the intermediate class, of which Love among others is a member. Wisdom is one of the most beautiful of things, and Love is love of beauty, so it follows that Love must be a lover of wisdom, and consequently in a state half-way between wisdom and ignorance. This too springs from the circumstances of his birth; his father was wise and fertile in expedients, his mother devoid of wisdom and helpless. So much for the nature of the spirit, my dear Socrates. As for your thinking as you did about Love, there is nothing remarkable in that; to judge by what you said, you identified Love with the beloved object instead of with what feels love; that is why you thought that Love is supremely beautiful. The object of love is in all truth beautiful and delicate and perfect and worthy to be thought happy, but what feels love has a totally different character such as I have just described."

' "Tell me then, my friend," I said, "for your words carry conviction, what function Love performs among men, if this is his nature." "That is precisely what I am going to try to teach you, Socrates. The nature and parentage of Love are as I have described, and he is also, according to you, love of beauty. But suppose we were to be asked: 'In what does love of beauty consist, Socrates and Diotima?' or, to put it more plainly, 'What is the aim of the love which is felt by the lover of beauty?' " "His aim is to attain possession of beautiful things," I answered. "But that merely raises a further question. What will have been gained by the man who is in possession of beauty?" I said that I could supply no ready answer to this question. "Well," she said, "let us change our terms and substitute good for beautiful. Suppose someone asked you: 'Now, Socrates, what is the aim of the love felt by the lover of the good?' " "Possession of the good," I replied. "And what will have been gained by the man who is in possession of the good?" "I find that an easier question to answer; he will be happy." "Presumably because happiness consists in the possession of the good, and once one has given that answer, the inquiry is at an end; there is no need to ask the further question 'Why does a man desire to be happy?' " "Quite so."

' "Now do you suppose that this desire and this love are characteristics common to all men, and that all perpetually desire to be in possession of the good, or what?" "That is exactly what I mean; they are common to all men." "Why is it then, Socrates, if all men are always in love with the same thing, that we do not speak of all men as being in love, but say that some men are in love and others not?" "I wonder what the reason can be." "There's no need to wonder; the truth is that we isolate a particular kind of love and appropriate for it the name of love, which really belongs to a wider whole, while we

employ different names for the other kinds of love."
"Can you give me another example of such a usage?"
"Yes, here is one. By its original meaning poetry means
simply creation, and creation, as you know, can take very
various forms. Any action which is the cause of a thing
emerging from non-existence into existence might be
called poetry, and all the processes in all the crafts are
kinds of poetry, and all those who are engaged in them
poets." "Yes." "But yet they are not called poets, but
have other names, and out of the whole field of poetry
or creation one part, which deals with music and metre,
is isolated and called by the name of the whole. This
part alone is called poetry, and those whose province is
this part of poetry are called poets." "Quite true." "It
is just the same with love. The generic concept embraces every desire for good and for happiness; that is
precisely what almighty and all-ensnaring love is. But
this desire expresses itself in many ways, and those with
whom it takes the form of love of money or of physical
prowess or of wisdom are not said to be in love or called
lovers, whereas those whose passion runs in one particular channel usurp the name of lover, which belongs to
them all, and are said to be lovers and in love." "There
seems to be truth in what you say," I remarked. "There
is indeed a theory," she continued, "that lovers are
people who are in search of the other half of themselves,
but according to my view of the matter, my friend, love
is not desire either of the half or of the whole, unless that
half or whole happens to be good. Men are quite willing
to have their feet or their hands amputated if they believe those parts of themselves to be diseased. The truth

is, I think, that people are not attached to what particularly belongs to them, except in so far as they can identify what is good with what is their own, and what is bad with what is not their own. The only object of men's love is what is good. Don't you agree?" "Certainly I do." "May we then say without qualification that men are in love with what is good?" "Yes." "But we must add, mustn't we, that the aim of their love is the possession of the good for themselves?" "Yes." "And not only its possession but its perpetual possession?" "Certainly." "To sum up, then, love is desire for the perpetual possession of the good." "Very true."

' "Now that we have established what love invariably is, we must ask in what way and by what type of action men must show their intense desire if it is to deserve the name of love. What will this function be? Can you tell me?" "If I could, Diotima, I should not be feeling such admiration for your wisdom, or putting myself to school with you to learn precisely this." "Well," she said, "I will tell you. The function is that of procreation in what is beautiful, and such procreation can be either physical or spiritual." "What you say needs an interpreter. I don't understand." "I will put it more plainly. All men, Socrates, have a procreative impulse, both spiritual and physical, and when they come to maturity they feel a natural desire to beget children, but they can do so only in beauty and never in ugliness.[27] There is something divine about the whole matter; in procreation and bringing to birth the mortal creature is endowed with a touch of immortality. But the process cannot take place in disharmony, and ugliness is out of harmony with everything divine, whereas beauty is in harmony with it. That is why Beauty is the goddess who presides over birth, and why, when a person in a state of desire comes into contact with beauty, he has a feeling of serenity and happy relaxation which make procreation possible. But, when ugliness is near, the effect is just the opposite; he frowns and withdraws gloomily into himself and re-coils and contracts and cannot unite with it, but has painfully to retain what is teeming within him. So a person in whom desire is already active is violently attracted towards beauty, because beauty can deliver its possessor from the severity of his pangs. The object of love, Socrates, is not, as you think, beauty." "What is it then?" "Its object is to procreate and bring forth in beauty." "Really?" "It is so, I assure you. Now, why is procreation the object of love? Because procreation is the nearest thing to perpetuity and immortality that a mortal being can attain. If, as we agreed, the aim of love is the perpetual possession of the good, it necessarily follows that it must desire immortality together with the good, and the argument leads us to the inevitable con-clusion that love is love of immortality as well as of the good."

'All this, then, I learnt on the various occasions on which Diotima spoke to me on the subject of love. One day she asked me: "What do you suppose, Socrates, to be the cause of this love and this desire? Look at the behaviour of all animals, both beasts and birds. When-ever the desire to procreate seizes them, they fall a prey to a violent love-sickness. Their first object is to achieve union with one another, their second to provide for their young; for these they are ready to fight however great the odds, and to die if need be, suffering starvation themselves and making any other sacrifice in order to secure the survival of their progeny. With men you might suppose such behaviour to be the result of rational calculation, but what cause is to be ascribed for the occurrence of such love among the beasts? Can you tell me?" I again confessed that I didn't know. "How can you expect ever to become an expert on the subject of love, if you haven't any ideas about this?" "I told you before, Diotima, that this is precisely why I have come to you. I know that I need a teacher. So tell me the cause of this and of all the other phenomena connected with love."

' "Well, if you believe that the natural object of love is what we have more than once agreed that it is, the answer won't surprise you. The same argument holds good in the animal world as in the human, and mortal nature seeks, as far as may be, to perpetuate itself and become immortal. The only way in which it can achieve this is by procreation, which secures the perpetual replacement of an old member of the race by a new. Even during the period for which any living being is said to live and to retain his identity – as a man, for example, is called the same man from boyhood to old age – he does not in fact retain the same attributes, although he is called the same person; he is always becoming a new being and undergoing a process of loss and reparation, which affects his hair, his flesh, his bones, his blood, and his whole body. And not only his body, but his soul as well. No man's character, habits, opinions, desires, pleasures, pains, and fears remain always the same; new ones come into existence and old ones disappear. What happens with pieces of knowledge is even more remarkable; it is not merely that some appear and others disappear, so that we no more retain our identity with regard to knowledge than with regard to the other things I have mentioned, but that each individual piece of knowledge is subject to the same process as we are ourselves. When we use the word recollection we imply by using it that knowledge departs from us; forgetting is the departure of knowledge, and recollection, by implanting a new impression in the place of that which is lost, preserves it, and gives it a spurious appearance of uninterrupted identity. It is in this way that everything mortal is preserved; not by remaining for ever the same, which is the prerogative of divinity, but by undergoing a process in which the losses caused by age are repaired by new acquisitions of a similar kind. This device, Socrates, enables the mortal to partake of immortality, physically as well as in other ways; but the immortal enjoys immortality after another manner. So do not feel surprise that every creature naturally cherishes its own progeny; it is in order to secure immortality that each individual is haunted by this eager desire and love.'

'I was surprised at this account and said: "You may be very wise, Diotima, but am I really to believe this?" "Certainly you are," she replied in true professional style; "if you will only reflect you will see that the ambition of men provides an example of the same truth.

You will be astonished at its irrationality unless you bear in mind what I have said, and remember that the love of fame and the desire to win a glory that shall never die have the strongest effects upon people. For this even more than for their children they are ready to run risks, spend their substance, endure every kind of hardships and even sacrifice their lives. Do you suppose that Alcestis would have died to save Admetus, or Achilles to avenge Patroclus, or your Codrus to preserve his kingdom for his sons,[28] if they had not believed that their courage would live for ever in men's memory, as it does in ours? On the contrary; it is desire for immortal renown and a glorious reputation such as theirs that is the incentive of all actions, and the better a man is, the stronger the incentive; he is in love with immortality. Those whose creative instinct is physical have recourse to women, and show their love in this way, believing that by begetting children they can secure for themselves an immortal and blessed memory hereafter for ever; but there are some whose creative desire is of the soul, and who long to beget spiritually, not physically, the progeny which it is the nature of the soul to create and bring to birth. If you ask what that progeny is, it is wisdom and virtue in general; of this all poets and such craftsmen as have found out some new thing may be said to be begetters; but far the greatest and fairest branch of wisdom is that which is concerned with the due ordering of states and families, whose name is moderation and justice. When by divine inspiration a man finds himself from his youth up spiritually fraught with these qualities, as soon as he comes of due age he desires to procreate and to have children, and goes in search of a beautiful object in which to satisfy his desire; for he can never bring his children to birth in ugliness. In this condition physical beauty is more pleasing to him than ugliness, and if in a beautiful body he finds also a beautiful and noble and gracious soul, he welcomes the combination warmly, and finds much to say to such a one about virtue and the qualities and actions which mark a good man, and takes his education in hand. By intimate association with beauty embodied in his friend, and by keeping him always before his mind, he succeeds in bringing to birth the children he has long desired to have, and once they are born he shares their upbringing with his friend; the partnership between them will be far closer and the bond of affection far stronger than between ordinary parents, because the children that they share surpass human children by being immortal as well as more beautiful. Everyone would prefer children such as these to children after the flesh. Take Homer, for example, and Hesiod, and the other good poets; who would not envy them the children that they left behind them, children whose qualities have won immortal fame and glory for their parents? Or take Lycurgus the lawgiver,[29] and consider the children that he left at Sparta to be the salvation not only of Sparta but one may almost say of Greece. Among you Athenians Solon is honoured for the laws which he produced,[30] and so it is in many other places with other men, both Greek and barbarian, who by their many fine actions have brought forth good fruit of all kinds; not a few of them have even won men's worship on account of their spiritual children, a thing which has never yet happened to anyone by reason of his human progeny.

' "So far, Socrates, I have dealt with love-mysteries into which even you could probably be initiated, but whether you could grasp the perfect revelation to which they lead the pilgrim if he does not stray from the right path, I do not know. However, you shall not fail for any lack of willingness on my part: I will tell you of it, and do you try to follow if you can.

' "The man who would pursue the right way to this goal must begin, when he is young, by applying himself to the contemplation of physical beauty, and, if he is properly directed by his guide, he will first fall in love with one particular beautiful person and beget noble sentiments in partnership with him. Later he will observe that physical beauty in any person is closely akin to physical beauty in any other, and that, if he is to make beauty of outward form the object of his quest, it is great folly not to acknowledge that the beauty exhibited in all bodies is one and the same; when he has reached this conclusion he will become a lover of all physical beauty, and will relax the intensity of his passion for one particular person, because he will realize that such a passion is beneath him and of small account. The next stage is for him to reckon beauty of soul more valuable than beauty of body; the result will be that, when he encounters a virtuous soul in a body which has little of the bloom of beauty, he will be content to love and cherish it and to bring forth such notions as may serve to make young people better; in this way he will be compelled to contemplate beauty as it exists in activities and institutions, and to recognize that here too all beauty is akin, so that he will be led to consider physical beauty taken as a whole a poor thing in comparison. From morals he must be directed to the sciences and contemplate their beauty also, so that, having his eyes fixed upon beauty in the widest sense, he may no longer be the slave of a base and mean-spirited devotion to an individual example of beauty, whether the object of his love be a boy or a man or an activity, but, by gazing upon the vast ocean of beauty to which his attention is now turned, may bring forth in the abundance of his love of wisdom many beautiful and magnificent sentiments and ideas, until at last, strengthened and increased in stature by this experience, he catches sight of one unique science whose object is the beauty of which I am about to speak. And here I must ask you to pay the closest possible attention.

' "The man who has been guided thus far in the mysteries of love, and who has directed his thoughts towards examples of beauty in due and orderly succession, will suddenly have revealed to him as he approaches the end of his initiation a beauty whose nature is marvellous indeed, the final goal, Socrates, of all his previous efforts. This beauty is first of all eternal; it neither comes into being nor passes away, neither waxes nor wanes; next, it is not beautiful in part and ugly in part, nor beautiful at one time and ugly at another, nor beautiful in this relation and ugly in that, nor beautiful here and ugly there, as varying according to its beholders; nor again will this beauty appear to him like the beauty of a face or hands or anything else corporeal, or like the beauty of a thought or a science, or like beauty which has its seat in something other than itself, be it a living thing or the earth or the sky or anything else whatever; he will see it as absolute, existing alone with itself, unique, eternal, and all other beautiful things as partaking of it, yet in such a manner that, while they come into being and pass away, it neither undergoes any increase or diminution nor suffers any change.

‘ "When a man, starting from this sensible world and making his way upward by a right use of his feeling of love for boys, begins to catch sight of that beauty, he is very near his goal. This is the right way of approaching or being initiated into the mysteries of love, to begin with examples of beauty in this world, and using them as steps to ascend continually with that absolute beauty as one's aim, from one instance of physical beauty to two and from two to all, then from physical beauty to moral beauty, and from moral beauty to the beauty of knowledge, until from knowledge of various kinds one arrives at the supreme knowledge whose sole object is that absolute beauty, and knows at last what absolute beauty is.

‘ "This above all others, my dear Socrates," the woman from Mantinea continued, "is the region where a man's life should be spent, in the contemplation of absolute beauty. Once you have seen that, you will not value it in terms of gold or rich clothing or of the beauty of boys and young men, the sight of whom at present throws you and many people like you into such an ecstasy that, provided that you could always enjoy the sight and company of your darlings, you would be content to go without food and drink, if that were possible, and to pass your whole time with them in the contemplation of their beauty. What may we suppose to be the felicity of the man who sees absolute beauty in its essence, pure and unalloyed, who, instead of a beauty tainted by human flesh and colour and a mass of perishable rubbish, is able to apprehend divine beauty where it exists apart and alone? Do you think that it will be a poor life that a man leads who has his gaze fixed in that direction, who contemplates absolute beauty with the appropriate faculty and is in constant union with it? Do you not see that in that region alone where he sees beauty with the faculty capable of seeing it, will he be able to bring forth not mere reflected images of goodness but true goodness, because he will be in contact not with a reflection but with the truth? And having brought forth and nurtured true goodness he will have the privilege of being beloved of God, and becoming, if ever a man can, immortal himself."

'This, Phaedrus and my other friends, is what Diotima said and what I believe; and because I believe it I try to persuade others that in the acquisition of this blessing human nature can find no better helper than Love. I declare that it is the duty of every man to honour Love, and I honour and practise the mysteries of Love in an especial degree myself, and recommend the same to others, and I praise the power and valour of Love to the best of my ability both now and always. There is my speech, Phaedrus; if you like, you can regard it as a panegyric delivered in honour of Love; otherwise you can give it any name you please.'

During the applause which followed the end of Socrates' speech Aristophanes, according to Aristodemus, was trying to explain that it was his theory that Socrates had referred to at one point, when suddenly there was a loud knocking at the street door. It sounded like a party of drunks; one could hear a girl playing the flute.

'Go and see who it is,' Agathon said to the servants, 'and if it is any of our friends ask them in. Otherwise say that my party is over and that we are going to bed.'

A moment later they heard the voice of Alcibiades in the courtyard, very tipsy and shouting, wanting to know where Agathon was and demanding to be taken to Agathon. He was helped in by the flute-girl and some of his other companions; he stood in the doorway crowned with a thick wreath of ivy and violets, from which a number of ribands hung about his head, and said:

'Good evening, gentlemen. Will you welcome into your company a man who is already drunk, utterly drunk, or shall we just put a garland on Agathon, which is what we came for, and go away? I couldn't be at the celebration yesterday, but I've come now with this wreath to have the pleasure of transferring it from my own head to the head of this paragon of beauty and cleverness. You'll laugh at me, will you, because I'm drunk? Well, you may laugh, but I know that what I say is true. But tell me at once, am I to join your party on the conditions stated? Will you drink with me or not?'

There was a unanimous cry that he should come in, and Agathon joined in the invitation. So in he came, supported by the people with him, and trying to take off the wreath with which he meant to crown Agathon. It was tilted over his eyes, and so he did not see Socrates, but sat down next to Agathon, with Socrates, who moved so as to make room for him, on his other side. As he took his place he embraced Agathon and crowned him.

'Take off Alcibiades' shoes,' ordered Agathon, 'so that he can put his feet up and make a third at this table.'

'Splendid,' said Alcibiades, 'but who is our table companion?' With these words he twisted himself round and saw Socrates, then leapt to his feet, and said: 'Good God, what have we here? Socrates? Lying there in wait for me again? How like you to make a sudden appearance just when I least expect to find you. What are you doing here? And why have you taken this place? You ought to be next to Aristophanes or some other actual or would-be buffoon, and instead you've managed to get yourself next to the handsomest person in the room.'

'Be ready to protect me, Agathon,' said Socrates, 'for I find that the love of this fellow has become no small burden. From the moment when I first fell in love with him I haven't been able to exchange a glance or a word with a single good-looking person without his falling into a passion of jealousy and envy, which makes him behave outrageously and abuse me and practically lay violent hands on me. See to it that he doesn't commit some excess even here, or if he attempts to do anything violent protect me; I am really quite scared by his mad behaviour and the intensity of his affection.'

'There can be no peace between you and me,' said Alcibiades, 'but I'll settle accounts with you for this

presently. For the moment, Agathon, give me some of
those ribands to make a wreath for his head too, for a
truly wonderful head it is. Otherwise he might blame
me for crowning you and leaving him uncrowned,
whose words bring him victory over all men at all times,
not merely on single occasions, like yours the day before
yesterday.' So saying he took some of the ribands, made
a wreath for Socrates, and lay back.

As soon as he had done so he exclaimed: 'Come, sirs,
you seem to me to be quite sober; this can't be allowed;
you must drink; it's part of our agreement. So as master
of the revels, until you are in adequate drinking order, I
appoint – myself. Let them bring a big cup, Agathon,
if you've got one. No, never mind, bring that wine-
cooler,' he went on, seeing one that held more than half
a gallon. He had this filled, and first of all drained it
himself, and then told them to fill it again for Socrates,
adding as he did so: 'Not that my scheming will have the
slightest effect on Socrates, my friends. He will drink
any quantity that he is bid, and never be drunk all the
same.' The servant refilled the vessel for Socrates, and
he drank.

Then Eryximachus began: 'This is no way for us to
be going on, Alcibiades. Are we to have neither conversation nor songs over our wine, but just to sit drinking as men do when they are thirsty?'

'Ah, Eryximachus,' replied Alcibiades, 'best of sons of
the best and soberest of fathers, my compliments to
you.'

'And mine to you,' said Eryximachus. 'But how are
we to amuse ourselves?'

'However you like; we must obey your orders. "One man of healing shall a host outweigh."[31] So prescribe for us whatever you choose.'

'Listen then,' said Eryximachus. 'Before you came we had resolved that each of us in turn, going from left to right, should make the best speech he could in praise of Love. The rest of us have already spoken, so it is clearly right that you, who have not yet spoken, but have finished your wine, should deliver a speech, and then prescribe whatever task you like to Socrates, and he to his right-hand neighbour, and so on.'

'An excellent idea, Eryximachus, but it can't be fair to make a man who is drunk compete in speaking with men who are sober. Besides, my good friend, you surely don't believe a word of what Socrates has just said? You know that the truth is quite the opposite? If I praise any person but him in his presence, be it god or man, he won't be able to keep his hands off me.'

'Be quiet,' said Socrates.

'It's no good your protesting,' Alcibiades said. 'I won't make a speech in praise of any other person in your presence.'

'Very well,' said Eryximachus, 'adopt that course, if you like, and make a speech in praise of Socrates.'

'What?' said Alcibiades. 'Do you think I ought, Eryximachus? Shall I set about the fellow and pay him out in the presence of you all?'

'Here, I say!' said Socrates; 'what have you in mind? Are you going to make fun of me by a mock-panegyric? Or what?'

'I shall tell the truth. Do you allow that?'

'Oh yes, I'll allow you to tell the truth; I'll even invite you to do so.'

'Very well then,' said Alcibiades. 'And here is what you can do. If I say anything untrue, pull me up in the middle of my speech, if you like, and tell me that I'm lying. I certainly shan't do so intentionally. But don't be surprised if I get into a muddle in my reminiscences; it isn't easy for a man in my condition to sum up your extraordinary character in a smooth and orderly sequence.

'I propose to praise Socrates, gentlemen, by using similes. He will perhaps think that I mean to make fun of him, but my object in employing them is truth, not ridicule. I declare that he bears a strong resemblance to those figures of Silenus[32] in statuaries' shops, represented holding pipes or flutes; they are hollow inside, and when they are taken apart you see that they contain little figures of gods. I declare also that he is like Marsyas the satyr.[33] You can't deny yourself, Socrates, that you have a striking physical likeness to both of these, and you shall hear in a moment how you resemble them in other respects. For one thing you're a bully, aren't you? I can bring evidence of this if you don't admit it. But you don't play the flute, you will say. No, indeed; the performance you give is far more remarkable. Marsyas needed an instrument in order to charm men by the power which proceeded out of his mouth, a power which is still exercised by those who perform his melodies (I reckon the tunes ascribed to Olympus to belong to Marsyas, who taught him); his productions alone, whether executed by a skilled male performer or by a wretched flute-girl, are capable, by reason of their divine origin, of throwing men into a trance and thus distinguishing those who yearn to enter by initiation into union with the gods. But you, Socrates, are so far superior to Marsyas that you produce the same effect by mere words without any instrument. At any rate, whereas we most of us pay little or no attention to the words of any other speaker, however accomplished, a speech by you or even a very indifferent report of what you have said stirs us to the depths and casts a spell over us, men and women and young lads alike. I myself, gentlemen, were it not that you would think me absolutely drunk, would have stated on oath the effect which his words have had on me, an effect which persists to the present time. Whenever I listen to him my heart beats faster than if I were in a religious frenzy, and tears run down my face, and I observe that numbers of other people have the same experience. Nothing of this kind ever used to happen to me when I listened to Pericles and other good speakers; I recognized that they spoke well, but my soul was not thrown into confusion and dismay by the thought that my life was no better than a slave's. That is the condition to which I have often been reduced by our modern Marsyas, with the result that it seems impossible to go on living in my present state. You can't say that this isn't true, Socrates. And even at this moment, I know quite well that, if I were prepared to give ear to him, I should not be able to hold out, but the same thing would happen again. He compels me to realize that I am still a mass of imperfections and yet persistently neglect my own true interests by engaging in public life. So against my real inclination I stop up my ears and take refuge in flight, as Odysseus did from the Sirens;[34] otherwise I should sit here beside him till I was an old man. He is the only person in whose presence I experience a sensation of which I might be thought incapable, a sensation of shame; he, and he alone, positively makes me ashamed of myself. The reason is that I am conscious that there is no arguing against the conclusion that one should do as he bids, and yet that, whenever I am away from him, I succumb to the temptations of popularity. So I behave like a runaway slave and take to my heels, and when I see him the conclusions which he has forced upon me make me ashamed. Many a time I should be glad for him to vanish from the face of the earth, but I know that, if that were to happen, my sorrow would far outweigh my relief. In fact, I simply do not know what to do about him.

'This is the effect which the "piping" of this satyr has had on me and on many other people. But listen and you shall hear how in other respects too he resembles the creatures to which I compared him; and how marvellous is the power which he possesses. You may be sure that none of you knows his true nature, but I will reveal him to you, now that I have begun. The Socrates whom you see has a tendency to fall in love with good-looking young men, and is always in their society and in an ecstasy about them. (Besides, he is, to all appearances, universally ignorant and knows nothing.) But this is exactly the point in which he resembles Silenus; he wears these characteristics superficially, like the carved figure, but once you see beneath the surface you will discover a degree of self-control of which you can hardly form a notion, gentlemen. Believe me, it makes no difference to him whether a person is good-looking – he despises good looks to an almost inconceivable extent – nor whether he is rich nor whether he possesses any of the other advantages that rank high in popular esteem; to him all these things are worthless, and we ourselves of no account, be sure of that. He spends his whole life pretending and playing with people, and I doubt whether anyone has ever seen the treasures which are revealed when he grows serious and exposes what he keeps inside. However, I once saw them, and found them so divine and precious and beautiful and marvellous that, to put the matter briefly, I had no choice but to do whatever Socrates bade me.

'Believing that he was serious in his admiration of my charms, I supposed that a wonderful piece of good luck had befallen me; I should now be able, in return for my favours, to find out all that Socrates knew; for you must know that there was no limit to the pride that I felt in my good looks. With this end in view I sent away my attendant, whom hitherto I had always kept with me in my encounters with Socrates, and left myself alone with him. I must tell you the whole truth; attend carefully, and do you, Socrates, pull me up if anything I say is false. I allowed myself to be alone with him, I say, gentlemen, and I naturally supposed that he would embark on conversation of the type that a lover usually addresses to his darling when they are *tête-à-tête*, and I was glad. Nothing of the kind; he spent the day with me in the sort of talk which is habitual with him, and then left me and went away. Next I invited him to train with me in the gymnasium, and I accompanied him there, believing that I should succeed with him now. He took exercise and wrestled with me frequently, with no one else present, but I need hardly say that I was no nearer my goal. Finding that this was no good either, I resolved to make a direct assault on him, and not to give up what I had once undertaken; I felt that I must get to the bottom of the matter. So I invited him to dine with me, behaving just like a lover who has designs upon his favourite. He was in no hurry to accept this invitation, but at last he agreed to come. The first time he came he rose to go away immediately after dinner, and on that occasion I was ashamed and let him go. But I returned to the attack, and this time I kept him in conversation after dinner far into the night, and then, when he wanted to be going, I compelled him to stay, on the plea that it was too late for him to go.

'So he betook himself to rest, using as a bed the couch on which he had reclined at dinner, next to mine, and there was nobody sleeping in the room but ourselves. Up to this point my story is such as might be told to anybody, but you would not have heard the sequel from me but for two reasons. In the first place there is, as the proverb says, truth in wine – whether one adds "and in children" or not is of no significance – and in the second it would be wrong, when one is setting out to compose a panegyric, to allow so proud an exploit on the part of Socrates to remain unknown. Besides, I am in much the same state as a man suffering from snake-bite. They say that such a man cannot endure to reveal his sufferings except to those who have experienced the like; they are the only people who will understand and make allowances if his agony drives him to outrageous speech and behaviour. Now I have suffered a bite more painful than that in the most sensitive part in which one can be bitten; I have been wounded and stung in my heart or soul or whatever you like to call it by philosophical talk which clings more fiercely than a snake when it gets a hold on the soul of a not ill-endowed young man. Seeing too that your company consists of people like Phaedrus, Agathon, Eryximachus, Pausanias, Aristodemus, as well as Aristophanes, not to mention Socrates himself, people who have all had your share in the madness and frenzy of philosophy – well, you shall all hear what happened. You will make allowances both for my actions then and for my words now. As for the servants and any other vulgar and uninitiated persons who may be present, they must shut their ears tight against what I am going to say.

'Well, gentlemen, when the light was out and the servants had withdrawn, I decided not to beat about the bush with him, but to tell him my sentiments boldly. I nudged him and said: "Are you asleep, Socrates?" "Far from it," he answered. "Do you know what I think?" "No, what?" "I think that you are the only lover that I have ever had who is worthy of me, but that you are afraid to mention your passion to me. Now, what I feel about the matter is this, that it would be very foolish of me not to comply with your desires in this respect as well as in any other claim that you might make either on my property or on that of my friends. The cardinal object of my ambition is to come as near perfection as possible, and I believe that no one can give me such powerful assistance towards this end as you. So the disapproval of wise men, which I should incur if I refused to comply with your wishes, would cause me far more shame than the condemnation of the ignorant multitude if I yielded to you."

'He listened to what I had to say, and then made a thoroughly characteristic reply in his usual ironical style: "You must be a very sharp fellow, my dear Alcibiades, if what you say about me is true, and I really have a power which might help you to improve yourself. You must see in me a beauty which is incomparable and far superior to your own physical good looks, and if, having made this discovery, you are trying to get a share of it by exchanging your beauty for mine, you obviously mean to get much the better of the bargain; you are trying to get true beauty in return for sham; in fact, what you are proposing is to exchange dross for gold. But look more closely, my good friend, and make quite sure that you are not mistaken in your estimate of my worth. A man's mental vision does not begin to be keen until his physical vision is past its prime, and you are far from having reached that point."

' "Well," I said, "I have done my part; what I have said represents my real sentiments and it is now for you to decide what you think best for me and for yourself."

' "Quite right," he answered, "we will consider hereafter, and do whatever seems to be best in this as in other matters."

'I had now discharged my artillery, and from the answer which he made I judged that I had wounded him; so, without allowing him to say anything further,

I got up and covered him with my own clothes – for it was winter – and then laid myself down under his worn cloak, and threw my arms round this truly superhuman and wonderful man, and remained thus the whole night long. Here again, Socrates, you cannot deny that I am telling the truth. But in spite of all my efforts he proved completely superior to my charms and triumphed over them and put them to scorn, insulting me in the very point on which I piqued myself, gentlemen of the jury – I may well call you that, since you have the case of Socrates' disdainful behaviour before you. I swear by all the gods in heaven that for anything that had happened between us when I got up after sleeping with Socrates, I might have been sleeping with my father or elder brother.

'What do you suppose to have been my state of mind after that? On the one hand I realized that I had been slighted, but on the other I felt a reverence for Socrates' character, his self-control and courage; I had met a man whose like for wisdom and fortitude I could never have expected to encounter. The result was that I could neither bring myself to be angry with him and tear myself away from his society, nor find a way of subduing him to my will. It was clear to me that he was more completely proof against bribes than Ajax against sword-wounds, and in the one point in which I had expected him to be vulnerable he had eluded me. I was utterly disconcerted, and wandered about in a state of enslavement to the man the like of which has never been known.

'It was after these events that we served in the campaign against Potidaea together, and were mess-mates there.[35] Of this I may say first that in supporting hardship he showed himself not merely my superior but the whole army's. Whenever we were cut off, as tends to happen on service, and compelled to go without food, the rest of us were nowhere in the matter of endurance. And again, when supplies were abundant, no one enjoyed them more; at drinking especially, though he drank only when he was forced to do so, he was invincible, and yet, what is most remarkable of all, no human being has ever seen Socrates drunk. You will see the proof of this very shortly if I am not mistaken. As for the hardships of winter – and the winters there are very severe – he performed prodigies; on one occasion in particular, when there was a tremendous frost, and everybody either remained indoors or, if they did go out, muffled themselves up in a quite unheard-of way, and tied and swathed their feet in felt and sheepskin, Socrates went out with nothing on but his ordinary clothes and without anything on his feet, and walked over the ice barefoot more easily than other people in their boots. The soldiers viewed him with suspicion, believing that he meant to humiliate them.

'So much for this subject, but "another exploit that the hero dared"[36] in the course of his military service is worth relating. A problem occurred to him early one day, and he stood still on the spot to consider it. When he couldn't solve it he didn't give up, but stood there ruminating. By the time it was midday people noticed him, and remarked to one another with wonder that Socrates had been standing wrapped in thought since early morning. Finally in the evening after dinner, some

Ionians brought their bedding outside – it was summer-time – where they could take their rest in the cool and at the same time keep an eye on Socrates to see if he would stand there all night as well. He remained standing until it was dawn and the sun rose. Then he made a prayer to the sun and went away.

'Now, if you please, we will consider his behaviour in battle; we ought to do him justice on this score as well. When the action took place in which I won my decoration for valour,[37] it was entirely to Socrates that I owed my preservation; he would not leave me when I was wounded, but succeeded in rescuing both me and my arms. That was the time too when I recommended the generals to confer the decoration on you, Socrates; here at any rate you cannot find any handle for criticism or contradiction. But the generals were influenced in my favour by the fact that I was well-connected, and their desire to confer the distinction on me was surpassed by your own eagerness that I should receive it rather than yourself. In addition, gentlemen, let me tell you that Socrates was a sight well worth seeing when the army made its disorderly retreat from Delium.[38] I was then serving in the cavalry, whereas he was an infantry-man, and after the rout had begun I came upon him marching along in company with Laches, and called out to them not to be down-hearted, and assured them that I would not desert them. And here I had an even better chance of observing Socrates than at Potidaea, because being mounted I had less occasion to be frightened myself. In the first place I noticed that he was far cooler than Laches, and next, if I may borrow an expression from you, Aristophanes, that he was using just the same gait as he does in Athens, "strutting along with his head in the air and casting side-long glances,"[39] quietly observing the movements of friend and foe, and making it perfectly plain even at a distance that he was prepared to put up a strong resistance to any attack. That is how both he and his companion got off safe; those who show a bold front in war are hardly ever molested; the attention of the pursuers is concentrated on those who are in headlong rout.

'One might find many other remarkable qualities to praise in Socrates, but a description of his general way of life would perhaps be equally applicable to some other people; the really wonderful thing about him is that he is like no other human being, living or dead. If you are looking for a parallel for Achilles, you can find it in Brasidas[40] and others; if Pericles is your subject you can compare him to Nestor and Antenor[41] (and they do not exhaust the possibilities); and you can make similar comparisons in other cases. But our friend here is so extraordinary, both in his person and in his conversation, that you will never be able to find anyone remotely resembling him either in antiquity or in the present generation, unless you go beyond humanity altogether, and have recourse to the images of Silenus and satyr which I am using myself in this speech. They are as applicable to his talk as to his person; I forgot to say at the beginning that his talk too is extremely like the Silenus-figures which take apart. Anyone who sets out to listen to Socrates talking will probably find his conversation utterly ridiculous at first, it is clothed in such curious words and phrases, the hide, so to speak, of a hectoring satyr. He will talk of pack-asses and black-smiths, cobblers and tanners, and appear to express the same ideas in the same language over and over again, so that any inexperienced or foolish person is bound to laugh at his way of speaking. But if a man penetrates within and sees the content of Socrates' talk exposed, he will find that there is nothing but sound sense inside, and that this talk is almost the talk of a god, and enshrines countless representations of ideal excellence, and is of the widest possible application; in fact that it extends over all the subjects with which a man who means to turn out a gentleman needs to concern himself.

'That is what I have to say, gentlemen, in praise of Socrates. I have included in my speech the grievance which I have against him, and told you how he has insulted me. I may add that I am not the only sufferer in this way; Charmides the son of Glaucon and Euthydemus the son of Diocles and many others have had the same treatment; he has pretended to be in love with them, when in fact he is himself the beloved rather than the lover. So I warn you, Agathon, not to be deceived by him; learn from my experience and be on your guard, and do not be like the child in the proverb, who learns to dread the fire by being burnt.'

When Alcibiades had finished, the freedom with which he had spoken raised a general laugh, because he seemed still to be amorously inclined towards Socrates. The latter took up the conversation and said: 'You seem to me quite sober, Alcibiades. Otherwise you wouldn't try to conceal your real object with such an apparatus of artful circumlocution, and then slip it in at the end by way of afterthought and as if the main motive of your whole speech were not to make trouble between Agathon and me. You think that I ought to be in love with nobody but you, and that nobody but you ought to be in love with Agathon. But we've seen through you; the object of your little play of satyr and Silenus is perfectly clear. Don't let him succeed, my dear Agathon; take steps to prevent anybody from setting you and me at variance.'

'You are very likely right, Socrates,' replied Agathon; 'no doubt that was why he sat down between us, in order to keep us apart. But he shan't succeed; I will come and take the place on your other side.'

'Do,' said Socrates; 'come and sit here, beyond me.'

'My God,' said Alcibiades, 'look how the fellow treats me. He thinks that he must always get the better of me. If you won't be content otherwise, you extra-ordinary man, you might at least let Agathon sit be-tween us.'

'Quite impossible,' said Socrates. 'You have just spoken in praise of me, and now it is my turn to speak in praise of my right-hand neighbour. If Agathon sits next to you, it will fall to him to speak in praise of me all over again, instead of my speaking in praise of him. Let it be as I propose, my good friend, and don't grudge the lad his tribute of praise from me, especially as I have a strong desire to eulogize him.'

'Hurrah, hurrah,' cried Agathon. 'You see I can't

stay here; I simply must change my place so as to have the privilege of being praised by Socrates.'

'That's just what always happens,' said Alcibiades. 'If Socrates is there no one else has a chance with anybody who is good-looking. See how readily he has found a plausible excuse for getting Agathon beside him.'

Agathon got up, intending to move to the place on the other side of Socrates. But at that moment a crowd of revellers came to the door, and finding it left open by somebody who had just gone out, made their way into the dining-room and installed themselves there. There was a general uproar, all order was abolished, and deep drinking became the rule.

Aristodemus reported that Eryximachus and Phaedrus and some others went away at this point. He himself fell asleep and slept for some time, as the nights were long at that time of year. Towards daybreak, when the cocks were already crowing, he woke up, and found that the rest of the party had either fallen asleep or gone away, and that the only people still awake were Agathon and Aristophanes and Socrates. They were drinking from a large cup which they passed round from left to right, and Socrates was holding forth to the others. Aristodemus did not remember most of what passed – he had not been conscious at the beginning of the conversation and was still nodding with sleep – but the main point was that Socrates was compelling them to admit that the man who knew how to write a comedy could also write a tragedy, and that a skilful tragic writer was capable of being also a comic writer. They were giving way to his arguments, which they didn't follow very well, and nodding. Aristophanes fell asleep first, and when it was fully light Agathon followed him.

Then Socrates, having put both his interlocutors to sleep, got up and went away, followed by Aristodemus, as usual. He went to the Lyceum[42] and washed, and spent the day as he would any other, and finally towards evening went home to bed.

NOTES ON THE TEXT

1. The original form of this proverb has been much debated. In the form in which it is given here there is a pun on the name of Agathon and *agathôn* (genitive plural of *agathos*, good). This gives a point to Socrates' remark which is unavoidably lost in English.

2. The guests at a Greek dinner-party reclined on the left elbow on couches which normally held two. Only women sat on chairs to dine, and respectable women would not be present at a party. The food was served on small movable tables. The place of honour was the left-hand place on the couch furthest to the left, and the right-hand couch would be occupied by the host. Agathon is alone at this till he is joined by Socrates on his right. When Alcibiades appears later and finds no room he reclines between them. The order in which these three are placed (Agathon – Alcibiades – Socrates) is of importance to the understanding of the final scene of the dialogue.

3. A symposium or drinking-party was distinct from the dinner which preceded it, and was conducted according to set rules. It generally included entertainment by professional musicians and dancers. Drinking was very formal, at any rate to begin with, and was regulated by the president, who prescribed the proportion of water to be mixed with the wine and the size of the draughts. This is the point of the discussion initiated by Pausanias. The three libations with which dinner ended correspond somewhat to a modern grace, and were offered to

Olympian Zeus, the Heroes, and Zeus the Saviour, and followed by a traditional song.

4. The professional educator or 'sophist' was a prominent figure in Greek life from about 450 B.C. onwards. He was normally an itinerant lecturer who moved from city to city giving for fees instruction in accomplishments which it behoved an educated and ambitious Greek gentleman to possess, such as the art of persuasive speech, literature, and conventional morality. The class included many famous men, such as Protagoras and Gorgias, who could command large sums and a great following. Socrates, though he professed to teach nothing and accepted no fees, was frequently confused with the Sophists in the popular mind. Plato is at great pains to correct this misunderstanding, and constantly stresses the contrast between the philosopher, whose object is truth and virtue, and the sophist, who aims merely at making his pupils successful in life, and who may be totally sceptical. The dialogue *Protagoras* contains satirical portraits of a number of sophists, including Prodicus of Ceos, and the attack on them is pressed with much more vehemence and bitterness in the *Gorgias* and the first book of the *Republic*.

5. Acusilaus of Argos was the author of a prose work called *Genealogies* on the origins of gods and men, which covered much the same ground as Hesiod's *Theogony*.

6. Parmenides (early 5th century B.C.), in obedience to what he believed to be strict logic, rejected the possibility of all plurality and change, and the line which is here quoted belongs to the fragmentary second part of his poem, in which he appears, in spite of his convictions, to have constructed a cosmogony of more or less traditional type. The context of the line is unknown.

7. It is possible that there is an allusion here to the famous *Sacred Band* of Thebes, which was organized on this

principle. It is first heard of under Epaminondas at Leuctra in 371 B.C., but may have been in existence somewhat before that date.

8. Admetus, king of Pherae in Thessaly, was told by Apollo that he must die unless he could induce a substitute to die in his place. When even his parents refused to do so his wife Alcestis offered herself. She was afterwards rescued from Hades by Heracles. The whole incident is the subject of Euripides' play *Alcestis*.

9. Orpheus was a mythical Thracian singer who, according to the familiar story, succeeded in rescuing his wife Eurydice from Hades, but lost her again by disregarding the injunction not to look back at her till they reached the upper air. He was subsequently torn in pieces by Dionysus' female worshippers in a religious frenzy. The version given here, which represents Orpheus' descent alive to hell as an act of cowardice rather than of courage, and his death as a punishment for this cowardice rather than for his disdain of Dionysus, is otherwise unknown and may be the product of Plato's own fancy.

10. The Islands of the Blest are reserved in Homer for certain favoured persons who do not share the fate of the majority, a shadow-life after death in the world below. They are conceived as actual places on the surface of the earth, somewhere in the western ocean, and life on them is described by Hesiod in the *Works and Days*. Achilles is not placed there by Homer, but other early writers admit him. Cf. Tennyson, *Ulysses*:

> 'It may be we shall touch the Happy Isles
> And see the great Achilles whom we knew.'

11. The argument is that the lover, being possessed by a god, deserves less credit for heroic actions than the beloved, because such possession makes it easier for him to perform them.

12. The distinction here drawn between two Aphrodites recurs in Xenophon's *Symposium*, where Socrates suggests that they may be essentially the same, though they have different titles and different temples. The existence of different temples is confirmed by the traveller Pausanias in the 2nd century A.D., but the exact significance of the title *Pandemos* (Common) is obscure. In any case the deductions drawn here about the natures of the two goddesses are presumably Plato's own.

13. The traditional myth taught that Aphrodite was born from the sea, into which had been thrown the severed members of her father Uranus when he was mutilated by his son Cronus.

14. Elis, Boeotia, and Sparta all belonged to the Dorian branch of the Greek race. Sparta, in particular, was notoriously given to homosexuality, possibly as a result of the barrack-room life to which her military organization confined her citizens. Boeotia was also celebrated for the slow-wittedness of its people.

15. Harmodius and his lover Aristogiton conspired in 514 B.C. to kill Hippias and Hipparchus, the sons of the late tyrant of Athens, Pisistratus. The plot was betrayed, and Hippias escaped, but later fell from power. Although the motive of the conspiracy appears to have been revenge for a personal insult, Harmodius and Aristogiton acquired immense posthumous fame as tyrannicides, and lived in the popular memory as classical examples of martyrs for liberty.

16. The belief that health consists in the maintenance of the proper proportion between the opposite constituents of the body is a commonplace of ancient medicine which can be traced back to Alcmaeon of Croton, a disciple of Pythagoras, and which survived into medieval times in the form of the doctrine of the four humours. When Eryximachus speaks of Asclepius as 'our forefather' he is

speaking as a member of one of the medical guilds which took the name of 'sons of Asclepius' from the name of the patron-god of medicine.

17. The reference to Heraclitus' 'unity which agrees with itself by being at variance' is to his doctrine that the universe and things in it are maintained in existence by the *simultaneous* operation of contrary tensions. His favourite illustration of this truth is a bow, in which contrary tensions are exerted at the same time by the bow and its string. Eryximachus' criticism completely misrepresents the whole theory of Heraclitus, who constantly asserted not only that opposites are necessarily co-existent and involve one another, but even that they are one and the same. Since Plato shows elsewhere that he was perfectly well aware of Heraclitus' meaning, his object here must be to satirize Eryximachus by making him guilty of a gross misinterpretation.

18. Much space is devoted by Plato in the *Republic* to the effect of various 'modes' in music upon the character of the hearer.

19. Ephialtes and Otus were giants who attempted to scale heaven by piling Mt Ossa on Mt Olympus and Mt Pelion on Mt Ossa. They were killed by Apollo.

20. It is almost certain that the reference here is to the punishment inflicted by the Spartans on Mantinea, an Arcadian city, in 385 B.C. The city was broken up and the inhabitants forced to live in four dispersed villages. Mention of this event in a conversation purporting to have taken place in 416 B.C. is of course an anachronism, but it provides valuable evidence for the date of composition.

21. Hesiod's *Theogony* describes such events, the mutilation of Uranus by Cronus, the imprisonment of the Cyclopes and hundred-armed giants, Cronus devouring his children, the war between Zeus and the Titans. There is no such

reference in the extant fragments of Parmenides, and the reading of his name here has been suspected.

22. A quotation from the rhetorician Alcidamas, a pupil of Gorgias.

23. A quotation from Sophocles' *Thyestes*.

24. A quotation from Euripides' *Stheneboea*.

25. The reference is to *Odyssey*, 11. 632. The Gorgon's head is introduced for the sake of the pun, but since its effect was to turn spectators to stone it is not inapposite. The artificialities of Agathon's style, especially the use of short parallel phrases at the end, are evidence that the speech is composed according to the precepts of Gorgias, the celebrated rhetorician and sophist.

26. Plato alludes to a line in Euripides' *Hippolytus*: 'My tongue has sworn, my mind remains unsworn,' which became a popular catchword and is employed with great effect against Euripides by Aristophanes in the *Frogs*.

27. Throughout the whole of the discussion which follows it must be borne in mind that such terms as 'conception', 'pregnancy', 'bringing forth' are used here in a quite general sense and without any reference to the specialized physical functions of male and female.

28. Codrus was a legendary king of Attica who in obedience to an oracle voluntarily sacrificed his life to save his country from a Dorian invasion.

29. Lycurgus was the figure to whom later generations ascribed the foundation of the Spartan constitutional and military system in the 9th century B.C., but his historical existence has been questioned. The reference to his system saving Greece is presumably to the part played by Sparta in the Persian wars.

30. Solon is unquestionably historical, though many legends collected round him. He was appointed to undertake the work of constitutional reform at Athens in the opening

decade of the 6th century B.C., and by his measures laid the foundations of the Athenian democracy.

31. Homer, *Iliad*, 11. 514.

32. Silenus, to whom Socrates was often compared in appearance, was the constant companion of Dionysus, and was represented as a bald, dissolute old man, with a flattened nose, generally riding upon an ass. In spite of his appearance and habits he was regarded as an inspired prophet, as in Virgil's *Sixth Eclogue*, and he is thus a suitable type of the wisdom which conceals itself beneath an uncouth exterior.

33. The Satyrs were also connected with Dionysus, and were beings with goat-like characteristics addicted to every kind of sensuality. Marsyas, one of their number, to whom, as well as to Silenus and Olympus, the invention of the flute was ascribed, challenged Apollo to a trial of skill in flute-playing, and on being defeated was flayed alive.

34. Odysseus, sailing past the island of the Sirens, who lured men to destruction by their songs, stopped his sailors' ears with wax and had himself bound to the mast, in order that he might hear the song and yet escape.

35. The refusal of Potidaea, a tributary of Athens in the peninsula of Chalcidice, to sever its connexion with Corinth, its mother-city, was one of the immediate causes of the Peloponnesian War. The siege of the city by the Athenians lasted over two years (432–430 B.C.), and ended in its capitulation.

36. Homer, *Odyssey*, 4.242.

37. The battle in which Alcibiades distinguished himself was the battle of Potidaea in 432 B.C., immediately before the blockade.

38. The battle of Delium in N.E. Boeotia took place in 424 B.C. The Athenians had seized and fortified it as part of a concerted attack on Boeotia, but in their withdrawal

they were seriously defeated by the Thebans under Pagondas.

39. The reference is to the description of Socrates' gait and expression in Aristophanes, *Clouds*, 362.

40. Brasidas, the most able and successful Spartan general in the first part of the Peloponnesian War, was killed at Amphipolis in 422 B.C.

41. Nestor and Antenor are the eloquent 'elder statesmen' on the Greek and Trojan side respectively in the *Iliad*.

42. The Lyceum was a gymnasium to which Socrates frequently resorted. Later it was used by Aristotle to teach in, and give its name to his school.

FOR THE BEST IN PAPERBACKS, LOOK FOR THE

In every corner of the world, on every subject under the sun, Penguins represent quality and variety – the very best in publishing today.

For complete information about books available from Penguin and how to order them, write to us at the appropriate address below. Please note that for copyright reasons the selection of books varies from country to country.

In the United Kingdom: For a complete list of books available from Penguin in the U.K., please write to *Dept EP, Penguin Books Ltd, Harmondsworth, Middlesex, UB7 0DA*

In the United States: For a complete list of books available from Penguin in the U.S., please write to *Dept BA, Viking Penguin, 299 Murray Hill Parkway, East Rutherford, New Jersey 07073*

In Canada: For a complete list of books available from Penguin in Canada, please write to *Penguin Books Canada Limited, 2801 John Street, Markham, Ontario L3R 1B4*

In Australia: For a complete list of books available from Penguin in Australia, please write to the *Marketing Department, Penguin Books Australia Ltd, P.O. Box 257, Ringwood, Victoria 3134*

In New Zealand: For a complete list of books available from Penguin in New Zealand, please write to the *Marketing Department, Penguin Books (N.Z.) Ltd, Private Bag, Takapuna, Auckland 9*

In India: For a complete list of books available from Penguin in India, please write to *Penguin Overseas Ltd, 706 Eros Apartments, 56 Nehru Place, New Delhi 110019*

PLATO

PROTAGORAS AND MENO

TRANSLATED BY W. K. C. GUTHRIE

Plato, the most brilliant of Socrates' pupils, held that philosophy must be a product of living contact between mind and mind, and his dialogues afforded him the means of reaching a wide audience. *Protagoras*, possibly his dramatic masterpiece, deals, like *Meno*, with the problem of teaching the art of successful living and good citizenship. While *Protagoras* keeps to the level of practical commonsense, *Meno* leads on into the heart of Plato's philosophy, the immortality of the soul and the doctrine that learning is knowledge acquired before birth.

THE LAST DAYS OF SOCRATES

TRANSLATED BY HUGH TREDENNICK

The trial and condemnation of Socrates, on charges of heresy and corrupting the minds of the young, forms one of the most tragic episodes in the history of Athens in decline. In the four works which compose this volume – *Euthyphro*, *The Apology*, *Crito*, and *Phaedo* – Plato, his most devoted disciple, has preserved for us the essence of his teaching and the logical system of question and answer he perfected in order to define the nature of virtue and knowledge. The vindication of Socrates and the pathos of his death are admirably conveyed in Hugh Tredennick's modern translation.

PLATO

TIMAEUS AND CRITIAS

TRANSLATED BY DESMOND LEE

The *Timaeus*, in which Plato attempted a scientific explanation of the universe's origin, is the earliest Greek account of a divine creation: as such it has significantly influenced European thought, even down to the present day. Yet this dialogue and, even more, its unfinished sequel, the *Critias*, have latterly attracted equal attention as the sources of the Atlantis legend. Plato's exact descriptions of an antediluvian world have fermented the imaginations of hundreds of writers in this century and the last, and the translator has now appended an intriguing survey of Atlantis and of theories (crazy and plausible) about the vanished continent.

GORGIAS

TRANSLATED BY WALTER HAMILTON

To judge by its bitter tone Plato's *Gorgias* was written shortly after the death of Socrates. Though Gorgias was a Sicilian teacher of oratory, the dialogue is more concerned with ethics than with the art of public speaking. The ability, professed particularly by the Sophists, to make the worse cause appear the better, struck Plato as the source of all corruption. The dialogue's chief interest lies, not in Gorgias' courteous outline of his art, but in the clash between Socrates, the true philosopher, and Callicles, a young Athenian of the stamp of Alcibiades, who brashly maintains that might is right.

PLATO

THE REPUBLIC

TRANSLATED BY DESMOND LEE

Plato, finally disillusioned by contemporary politics after the execution of Socrates, showed in his writings the enormous influence of that great philosopher. *The Republic*, his treatise on an ideal state, was the first of its kind in European thought. For Plato, political science was the science of the soul, and included moral science. *The Republic*'s emphasis on the right education for rulers, the prevalence of justice, and harmony between all classes of society, is as strong as its condemnation of democracy, which Plato considered encouraged bad leadership.

THE LAWS

TRANSLATED BY T. J. SAUNDERS

The reader of *The Republic*, Plato's best-known political work, may well be astonished by *The Laws*. Instead of an ideal state ruled directly by moral philosphers, this later work depicts a society permeated by the rule of law. Immutable laws control most aspects of public and private life, from civil and legal administration to marriage, religion and sport. The rigours of life in Plato's utopian Republic are not much tempered here, but *The Laws* is a much more practical approach to Plato's ideal.

Also published :

PHAEDRUS AND LETTERS VII AND VIII

A selection

Leo Tolstoy
THE KREUTZER SONATA AND OTHER STORIES
Translated by David McDuff

Propertius
THE POEMS
Translated by W. G. Shepherd and Introduced by Betty Radice

Henry Mayhew
LONDON LABOUR AND THE LONDON POOR
Selected and Introduced by Victor Neuburg

Soren Kierkegaard
FEAR AND TREMBLING
Translated by Alistair Hannay

Henry James
AN INTERNATIONAL EPISODE AND OTHER STORIES
Edited by S. Gorley Putt
SELECTIONS FROM THE CARMINA BURANA
Translated by David Parlett

Fyodor Dostoyevsky
THE HOUSE OF THE DEAD
Translated by David McDuff
SEVEN VIKING ROMANCES
Translated by Hermann Pálsson and Paul Edwards